T H E
10
Most Important
Things You
Can Say to a
JEHOVAH'S
WITNESS

RON RHODES

ERS

Cover by Terry Dugan Design, Minneapolis, Minnesota

THE 10 MOST IMPORTANT THINGS YOU CAN SAY TO A JEHOVAH'S WITNESS

Copyright © 2001 Ron Rhodes
Published by Harvest House Publishers
Eugene, Oregon 97402
www.harvesthousepublishers.com

Library of Congress Cataloging-in-Publication Data
Rhodes, Ron.
    The 10 most important things you can say to a Jehovah's Witness / Ron Rhodes.
        p. cm. — (The 10 most important things series)
    Includes bibliographical references.
    ISBN-13: 978-0-7369-0535-0
    ISBN-10: 0-7369-0535-9
    1. Jehovah's Witnesses—Controversial literature. 2. Witness bearing (Christianity) 3. Apologetics. I. Title: Ten most important things you can say to a Jehovah's Witness. II. Title. III. Series.

BX8526.5 .R55 2001
289.9'2—dc21   2001024085

This book is dedicated to the countless Christians across America who hold full-time jobs, have families to take care of at home, and are very busy in life's various endeavors—yet still desire to become equipped to defend the truth of Christianity against errant teaching. May this little book assist you in reaching that worthy goal!

Acknowledgments

A special thanks to the staff at Harvest House Publishers for coming up with the idea for this concise treatment on the Jehovah's Witnesses. All of us agree there is a real need for such a book.

I also want to take this opportunity to thank the thousands of people who contacted me following the publication of my earlier book, *Reasoning from the Scriptures with the Jehovah's Witnesses* (a considerably longer book—supplementary to the present volume—that is available in Christian bookstores). Your words of encouragement and your commitment to the cause of apologetics among cultists has been an inspiration to me.

Most of all, as always, I give heartfelt thanks to my wife, Kerri, and two children, David and Kylie, without whose support it would truly be impossible for me to do what I do.

Contents

Introduction 7

Icon Chart 9

1. The Watchtower Society Does Not
   Speak for God 11

2. The New World Translation Is Inaccurate and
   Misleading 23

3. God Has Other Names Besides Jehovah 33

4. Jesus Is God Almighty 41

5. The Holy Spirit Is God, Not a "Force" 55

6. The Biblical God Is a Trinity 63

7. Salvation Is by Grace Through Faith, Not by
   Works 73

8. There Is One People of God—Not Two Peoples
   with Different Destinies 85

9. Man Is Conscious in the Afterlife, and Hell
   Is a Real Place of Eternal Suffering 99

10. Jesus Changed My Life Forever 111

Bibliography 124

Notes 126

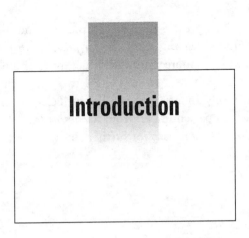

Introduction

This book is short on purpose. The chapters in this book are short on purpose. I believe there is something to be said for brevity. However, and I want to emphasize this very strongly, *brevity should not be thought of as shallow.* Focusing on ten critical points to share with your Jehovah's Witness friends, this book provides you with the most important apologetic information in the briefest possible fashion. In a day of information overload, the merits of such an approach are obvious.

Each chapter addresses an important issue to raise with Jehovah's Witnesses and includes supportive arguments to substantiate that particular issue. My desire is that you not only have the necessary information to "hold your own" in conversing with Jehovah's Witnesses on the doorstep, but that you would also become equipped to lead the Jehovah's Witness to the true God, the true Jesus, and the true gospel of grace. I pray that God uses you to bring Jehovah's Witnesses out of the kingdom of darkness and into the kingdom of light—the kingdom of Jesus Christ (see Colossians 1:13,14).

If the concise information in this book causes you to want to go deeper and learn even more about interacting with Jehovah's

Witnesses, that's great! I urge you to pick up and dig into my larger volume, *Reasoning from the Scriptures with the Jehovah's Witnesses*, which is more than three times the length of the book you are holding in your hands. These two books complement each other nicely. In fact, at the end of each chapter in this book are the relevant page numbers from *Reasoning from the Scriptures with the Jehovah's Witnesses* for further study.

Icons Used in this Book

To make this informative guide easier to follow and understand, the following icons highlight specific sections.

 Watchtower Society's position on a particular doctrine

 Key points to remember regarding the Watchtower's position

 The biblical position

 An important point

 Taking a closer look

 A witnessing tip

 Proceed with caution

 Quick-review checklist

 Digging deeper

If you run into witnessing trouble, feel free to contact Reasoning from the Scriptures Ministries. We will help you if we can.

Ron Rhodes
Reasoning from the Scriptures Ministries
P.O. Box 2526
Frisco, TX 75034
Phone: 214-853-4370

Email: ronrhodes@earthlink.net
Web: www.ronrhodes.org

Free newsletter available upon request.

1

The Watchtower Society
Does Not Speak for God

The Watchtower Society is the organization that governs Jehovah's Witnesses worldwide. Jehovah's Witnesses believe God personally set up this organization as His visible representative on earth. It is through this organization—*and no other*—that God allegedly teaches the Bible to humankind today. According to the Watchtower Society, people are unable to ascertain the true meaning of Scripture without its vast literature.

Jehovah's Witnesses are extremely exclusivistic in viewing the Watchtower Society as the sole possessor and propagator of God's truth. Other Christian organizations are viewed as deceptive and rooted in the work of the devil. Even reading the Bible is considered insufficient in and of itself in learning the things of God. Unless a person is in touch with the Watchtower Society, it is claimed, he or she will not progress spiritually even if that person reads the Bible regularly.[1] Witnesses are expected to obey the Society as the voice of God.[2] Not surprisingly, Watchtower literature is replete with admonitions to "dependent" Bible interpretation—that is, *dependent on the Watchtower Society*.[3]

If a Jehovah's Witness disobeys the instructions of the Watchtower Society—even on a relatively minor matter—the assumption is that this individual is apostate, and the punishment is disfellowshiping. Jehovah's Witnesses in good standing with the Watchtower Society are forbidden to interact or talk with one who has been disfellowshiped. The only exception to this is if the disfellowshiped person is in one's immediate family, such as a husband or wife, in which case it is permissible to conduct "necessary business."[4] The fear of disfellowshiping is one of the Watchtower's most effective means of keeping individual Jehovah's Witnesses obedient to its teachings.

The Watchtower Society

- The Watchtower Society is viewed as God's voice on earth.

- Jehovah's Witnesses are expected to unquestioningly obey the Watchtower.

- Witnesses are instructed to depend on the Watchtower for the correct interpretation of the Bible.

- Reading the Bible alone, without Watchtower literature, will lead a person astray.

- The penalty for failing to obey the Watchtower is disfellowshiping.

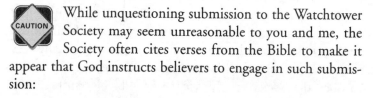

While unquestioning submission to the Watchtower Society may seem unreasonable to you and me, the Society often cites verses from the Bible to make it appear that God instructs believers to engage in such submission:

- Jehovah's Witnesses are taught that the Watchtower Society is the "faithful and discreet slave" mentioned by Jesus in Matthew 24:45-47 (NWT). Other Christian organizations are said to be represented by the evil slave mentioned in verses 48-51.[5]

- Jehovah's Witnesses are taught that the primary teaching of 2 Peter 1:20,21 is that there should be "no private interpretations" of the Bible. Only the Watchtower Society can offer the true meaning of the Bible.[6]

- The Watchtower Society cites Acts 8:30,31 [where Philip helps an Ethiopian man understand the Scriptures] to illustrate that people cannot rightly understand the Bible without an organization to guide them. The Watchtower is allegedly God's Bible-interpreting organization on earth.[7]

Below I will take a closer look at these verses.

 The Bible yields clear proof that the Watchtower Society is a human institution that does not speak for God. The Society 1) misinterprets key verses in supporting its own authority; 2) has a track record of false prophecies; and 3) has changed its position on important issues through the years—something that a true spokesman for God would never do. Consider the evidence.

 The Watchtower Society misinterprets key Scripture verses in supporting its own authority—especially Matthew 24:45-47; 2 Peter 1:20,21; and Acts 8:30,31.

Matthew 24:45-51

Who then is the faithful and wise servant, whom the master has put in charge of the servants in his household to give them their food at the proper time? It will be good for that servant whose master finds him doing so when he returns. I tell you the truth, he will put him in charge of all his possessions. But suppose that servant is wicked and says to himself, "My master is staying away a long time," and he then begins to beat his fellow servants and to eat and drink with drunkards. The master of that servant will come on a day when he does not expect him and at an hour he is not aware of. He will cut him to pieces and assign him a place with the hypocrites, where there will be weeping and gnashing of teeth.

The Watchtower Society *is not* the "faithful and wise servant" of which Jesus speaks in this passage. Jehovah's Witnesses are practicing *eisogesis* (reading a meaning into the text) instead of practicing *exegesis* (deriving the meaning out of the text).

Contrary to the Watchtower view, Jesus in this parable likens *any* follower to a servant who has been put in charge of his master's household. He contrasts two possible ways that each professed disciple could carry out the task—faithfully or unfaithfully. The servant who chooses to be faithful makes every effort and focuses all his energies on fulfilling his commitments and obligations while his master is away. By contrast, the unfaithful servant calculates that his master will be away for a prolonged time and decides to mistreat his fellow servants and "live it up." He is careless and callous, utterly failing to fulfill his obligations. *Jesus' message is a call to every Christian to be faithful.* Those who are faithful will be rewarded at the Lord's return.

 Since the Watchtower Society claims to be God's collective faithful slave that alone guides people in their understanding of Scripture, and since this organization did not come into existence until the late-nineteenth century, does this mean God had no true representatives on earth for many centuries? Does this mean God did not care whether people understood the Bible for all those centuries? Ask your Jehovah's Witness friend.

2 Peter 1:20,21

The Jehovah's Witnesses' New World Translation renders verse 20: "For you know this first, that no prophecy of Scripture springs from any private interpretation." Contrary to the Watchtower understanding, the word "interpretation" here literally means "unloosing" in the Greek.[8] The verse could be paraphrased: "No prophecy of Scripture is a matter of one's own *unloosing*." In other words, the prophecies did not stem merely from the prophets themselves or by human imaginings, but ultimately they came *from* God (as verse 21 goes on to emphatically state). This passage is not dealing with how to *interpret* Scripture but rather deals with how Scripture *came to be written*.[9]

With this in mind, let us consider verses 20 and 21 together: "But know this first of all, that no prophecy of Scripture is a matter of one's own [unloosing], *for* no prophecy was ever made by an act of human will, but men moved by the Holy Spirit spoke from God" (NASB, emphasis added). Now, the word "for" at the beginning of verse 21 ("*for* no prophecy was ever made by...") carries an *explanatory* function, indicating that verse 21 *explains* verse 20 by restating its contents and then pointing to God as the author of Scripture. This means verse 21 contextually indicates that the *collective focus* of verses 20 and 21 is Scripture's *origin*, not its *interpretation*.

The Holy Spirit's Role

The Word "moved" in 2 Peter 1:21 NASB ("men *moved* by the Holy Spirit spoke from God") literally means "borne along" or "carried along." Luke uses this word to refer to a ship being "borne along" by the wind (Acts 27:15,17). The experienced sailors on the ship could not navigate the ship because the wind was so strong. The ship was being *driven* by the wind. Likewise, the biblical authors were driven, directed, and carried by the Holy Spirit.

The Holy Spirit "moved" or "directed" the human authors of the Bible as they wrote (2 Peter 1:21). The word "moved" is a strong one, indicating the Spirit's complete superintendence of the human authors. While humans were individually active and consciously involved in writing Scripture, the Spirit ultimately directed them in what they wrote. In view of this, 2 Peter 1:20,21 cannot be used to support the Watchtower's contention that people should avoid "private interpretations" of what Scripture means. Such an interpretation is foreign to the context.

Acts 8:30,31

> Then Philip ran up to the chariot and heard the man reading Isaiah the prophet. "Do you understand what you are reading?" Philip asked. "How can I," he said, "unless someone explains it to me?" So he invited Philip to come up and sit with him.

On the one hand, this passage indicates that guidance is *sometimes* needed to help people understand Scripture. The meaning of certain Scripture passages is not always immediately evident, even to those who are earnest seekers. This is one reason God gives "teachers" to the church (see Ephesians 4:11) and provides the illuminating ministry of the Holy Spirit (John 16:12-15).

However, there is no evidence for an organization whose infallible views must be accepted by all true followers of God. In Acts 8:30,31, *one man* (Philip) taught an Ethiopian man *directly from Scripture* (not from literature designed by an organization), after which time the Ethiopian confessed his faith in Christ and got baptized (see Acts 8:34-38).

 The Bible tells us that when Philip and the Ethiopian "came up out of the water, the Spirit of the Lord snatched Philip away; and *the eunuch no longer saw him*, but went on his way rejoicing" (Acts 8:39 NASB, emphasis added). The eunuch did not have to join and submit to an organization. Drive this point home to your Jehovah's Witness friend.

 Contrary to biblical prophets, the Watchtower Society has a track record of giving false prophecies. Although claiming to be a "prophet" organization, the Watchtower Society has set forth false prophecies. Three of them are especially notable:

- The Watchtower Society (WS) predicted that 1914 would mark the overthrow of human governments and the full establishment of God's kingdom on earth.[10]

- The WS predicted that in 1925 select Old Testament saints (Abraham, Isaac, and Jacob) would rise from the grave and live in San Diego.[11]

- The WS predicted that in 1975 human history would end and the 1,000-year reign of Christ would begin.[12]

 False Prophecies in Watchtower Literature

1914: *Studies in the Scriptures* (1891) refers to "the full establishment of the Kingdom of God in the earth at A.D. 1914."

1925: *Millions Now Living Will Never Die* (1920) said, "1925 will mark the return of Abraham, Isaac, Jacob, and the faithful prophets of old."

1975: *Our Kingdom Ministry* (in 1968) claimed: "There are only about ninety months [7½ years] left before 6,000 years of man's existence on earth is completed."

Jehovah's Witnesses sometimes argue that some of the biblical prophets held mistaken views and yet they were not branded as false prophets. Jonah is cited as an example. Jonah's prediction about the destruction of Nineveh did not come to pass (see Jonah 3:4-10; 4:1,2). Clearly, we are told, a biblical prophet made a mistake. Since Jonah was not condemned, neither should modern "prophet" organizations like the Watchtower Society be condemned for mistakes.

A look at the Bible, however, proves that Jonah did not make a mistake. Indeed, he told the Ninevites *precisely* what God had told him to say (Jonah 3:1). Since God cannot err (Hebrews 6:18; Titus 1:2), Jonah's statement was not a false prophecy. It is clear that there was an implied condition in Jonah's exhortation to Nineveh: *"Unless you repent,* God will destroy you." The fulfillment of the threat of judgment was thus contingent on the repentance of Nineveh—a fact proven by their repentance (see 3:5) as well as by Jonah's selfish admission that he was afraid from the beginning that they would repent and God would save them (Jonah 4:2).

 God's allowance of repentance in the face of judgment is stated as a principle in Jeremiah 18:7,8: "If at any time I announce that a nation or kingdom is to be uprooted, torn down and destroyed, and if that nation I warned repents of its evil, then I will relent and not inflict on it the disaster I had planned." This principle is illustrated in the case of Nineveh. Thus, Jonah's prophecy cannot be cited to lessen the guilt of the Watchtower Society in its numerous false predictions. Biblical prophets were 100-percent accurate. If a prophet made a false prophecy, he was stoned to death (Deuteronomy 18:22). Emphasize this fact to the Jehovah's Witness.

The Watchtower Society has changed its position on important issues, something a true spokesman for God would never do. This charge is illustrated in the fact that the Watchtower Society (WS) has often changed its position on medical issues. Vaccinations are a good example. Back in 1931, the *Golden Age* magazine said that a "vaccination is a direct violation of the everlasting covenant that God made with Noah after the flood."[13] Vaccinations were forbidden by the WS for 20 years. However, it dropped this prohibition in the 1950s. The August 22, 1965 issue of *Awake!* magazine even acknowledged that vaccinations seem to have caused a decrease in diseases.[14] [Doesn't it make you wonder how parents of children who had died as a result of *not* being vaccinated in those early years felt when the WS (the "voice of God") suddenly reversed its position?]

We find another example in the Watchtower Society's change of position on organ transplants.[15] The November 15, 1967 issue of *The Watchtower* magazine said organ transplants amounted to cannibalism and are not appropriate for Christians.[16] The next year's issue of *Awake!* magazine agreed that *all* organ transplants are cannibalism.[17] The WS banned organ transplants for some 13 years, during which time many Jehovah's Witnesses died or suffered greatly as a result of not having such treatment. But the WS changed its position when the medical benefits of transplants became a proven fact. The March 15, 1980 issue of *The Watchtower* magazine said organ transplants are *not necessarily* cannibalistic[18] and began allowing them.

In view of such changes through the years, the Watchtower Society's claim to be the voice of God on earth is a shallow one. It is clear that the Society is a human institution that does not truly speak for God.

It is also worth noting that during the Watchtower presidency of Frederick Franz (1977–1992), there developed a crisis within the Watchtower Society as many Witnesses began to personally examine the history of the Society.[19] Some of those raising questions were prominent leaders who were soon forced out of the Watchtower organization for their disloyalty. One of these was Raymond Franz, former Governing Body member of the Watchtower Society and nephew of the president—an event newsworthy enough that *Time* magazine ran a full-page article about it.[20] Raymond, after being disfellowshiped, later affirmed that service on the Governing Body of the Watchtower Society was truly disillusioning, which he documented in a book called *Crisis of Conscience*. He demonstrated that the Society is not biblical, has uttered false prophecies, has altered key teachings and policies, and has participated in lying and cover-ups.[21] (Though *Crisis of Conscience* is not a Christian book, it does provide plenty of information against the Watchtower Society. You might consider reading it.)

Jehovah's Witnesses consider *Crisis of Conscience* to be "apostate literature" since it was written by a former Witness. Use the book to gather important information, but do not hand it to them on the doorstep. They will not read it.

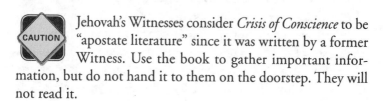

The Bible instructs us to test truth claims by Scripture, not by an external organization such as the Watchtower Society. Acts 17:11, for example, encourages us to follow the lead of the Bereans by testing religious claims against the Bible. They knew that the Bible is the only measuring stick for truth: "The Bereans...received the message with great eagerness and examined the Scriptures every day to see if what Paul said was true."

A key Bible passage that relates to this is 2 Timothy 3:15-17. The apostle Paul notes "how from infancy you [Timothy] have known the holy Scriptures, which are able to make you wise for salvation through faith in Christ Jesus. All Scripture is God-breathed and is useful for teaching, rebuking, correcting and training in righteousness, so that the man of God may be thoroughly equipped for every good work." Jewish boys formally began studying the Old Testament Scriptures when they were five years of age. Timothy had been taught the Scriptures by his mother and grandmother beginning at this age. And *Scripture alone* was sufficient to provide Timothy the necessary wisdom that leads to salvation through faith in Christ. The *Scriptures alone* are the ultimate source of spiritual knowledge.

Notice that 2 Timothy 3:16,17 does not tell us that Scripture *as seen through the lens of the Watchtower Society* is "useful for teaching, rebuking, correcting," and so forth. It is Scripture alone that does these things. And the reason Scripture can do these things is that "all Scripture is inspired by God" (verse 16). The word "inspired" means "God-breathed." Scripture is sufficient because its source is God. Watchtower literature, by contrast, comes from human wisdom.

The Watchtower Society Does Not Speak for God

✓ The Watchtower Society (WS) misinterprets Bible verses to support its authority.

✓ Unlike biblical prophets, the WS has a history of false prophecies.

✓ The WS has changed its position on important issues through the years.

✓ The Bible says to test all truth claims by *Scripture alone.*

For further facts on the Watchtower Society as a human institution that does not truly speak for God, I invite you to consult my book *Reasoning from the Scriptures with the Jehovah's Witnesses*, pp. 23-48, 339-75.

The New World Translation
Is Inaccurate and Misleading

During the Watchtower Society presidency of Nathan Knorr (1942–1977), the New World Translation (NWT) was produced and published. This translation was written to "restore" the name Jehovah in the Old Testament where the Hebrew consonants "YHWH" appear. This name is also inserted in the New Testament where the text refers to the Father (237 times). This was done despite the fact that it contradicts what is found in thousands of available Greek manuscripts of the New Testament.

Jehovah's Witnesses believe the New World Translation is the best translation available today. They also believe that because they are the only group that refers to God by His "true" name, Jehovah, they are the only true followers of God.

The New World Translation

- The New World Translation inserts "Jehovah" throughout both the Old and New Testaments.
- The Watchtower Society claims it is the best translation available today.

- Jehovah's Witnesses believe they are the only ones to use God's proper name, so they alone are true followers of God.

 The New World Translation is inaccurate, misleading, and heavily biased in favor of Watchtower Society theology. Indeed, this translation is worded in such a way that it virtually strips Jesus of His absolute deity. (Chapter 4 focuses on the Jehovah's Witness view of Jesus.) The Watchtower Society teaches that the Father is God Almighty while Jesus is a *lesser* god.

Since Jehovah's Witnesses who show up on your doorstep will likely cite the New World Translation, it is critical that you be aware of—and be able to refute—some of the distortions within its pages. More specifically, you should be able to 1) verbalize what legitimate biblical linguists say about the New World Translation; 2) demonstrate that the translators of the New World Translation were not biblical linguists; 3) show that the New World Translation has gone through major changes through the years; and 4) give specific examples of how the New World Translation has mistranslated key verses to support Watchtower Society theology.

Respected biblical linguists have given a universal "thumbs down" to the New World Translation. Consider:

- Dr. Julius Mantey, author of *A Manual Grammar of the Greek New Testament*, calls the New World Translation "a shocking mistranslation."[1]

- Dr. Bruce M. Metzger, late professor of New Testament at Princeton University, calls the New World Translation "a frightful mistranslation," "erroneous," "pernicious," and "reprehensible."[2]

- Dr. William Barclay asserted that "the deliberate distortion of truth by this sect is seen in their New Testament translation....It is abundantly clear that a sect which can translate the New Testament like that is intellectually dishonest."[3]

- Dr. Robert Countess, who wrote a doctoral dissertation on the Greek of the New World Translation, concluded that the translation "has been sharply unsuccessful in keeping doctrinal considerations from influencing the actual translation....It must be viewed as a radically biased piece of work. At some points it is actually dishonest. At others it is neither modern nor scholarly."[4]

- British scholar Dr. H.H. Rowley asserted, "From beginning to end this volume is a shining example of how the Bible should not be translated."[5] Rowley also said this translation is "an insult to the Word of God."[6]

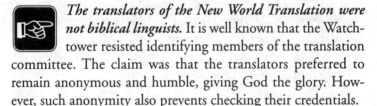 ***The translators of the New World Translation were not biblical linguists.*** It is well known that the Watchtower resisted identifying members of the translation committee. The claim was that the translators preferred to remain anonymous and humble, giving God the glory. However, such anonymity also prevents checking their credentials.

When high-level defector Raymond Franz, in his book *Crisis of Conscience*, finally revealed the identity of the translators—Nathan Knorr, Frederick Franz, Albert Schroeder, George Gangas, and Milton Henschel[7]—it quickly became apparent that the committee was unqualified for the task. Four of the five men in the committee had no Hebrew or Greek training whatsoever. In fact, they had only high school educations. The fifth—Frederick Franz—claimed to know Hebrew and Greek, but upon examination under oath in a court of law in Edinburgh, Scotland, he failed a simple Hebrew test.[8] Franz dropped out of the University of Cincinnati after his sophomore year. Even while there, he had not been studying anything related to theological issues.

Major changes have been made in the New World Translation through the years. An example is the Watchtower Society's position on worshiping Jesus. Early in its history, the Watchtower Society endorsed the worship of Jesus. An early issue of *The Watchtower* magazine (1880) said that "to worship Christ in any form cannot be wrong."[9] Some years later, another issue of the magazine (1892) said, "Yes, we believe our Lord Jesus while on earth was really worshipped, and properly so. While he was not *the* God, Jehovah, he was *a* God."[10]

In 1959, *The Watchtower* magazine changed its story and warned: "Do not erroneously conclude that Christians are to worship Christ; that is not what he taught."[11] In 1964, *The Watchtower* magazine dogmatically stated that "it is unscriptural for worshipers of the living and true God to render worship to the Son of God, Jesus Christ."[12]

This change in doctrine is reflected in the Jehovah's Witnesses' New World Translation. The 1961 edition of the book translated Hebrews 1:6: "But when he again brings his Firstborn into the inhabited earth, he says: 'And let all God's angels *worship* him'" (emphasis added). By contrast, the 1971 edition reads: "But when he again brings his Firstborn into the inhabited earth, he says: 'And let all God's angels *do obeisance* to him'" (emphasis added).

 Point out that the 1961 edition of the New World Translation renders Hebrews 1:6 to say that angels should *worship* Jesus, while the 1971 edition says angels should merely respect or submit to Him. Help your Jehovah's Witness acquaintance see that he or she is basing salvation on a translation that is *evolving* based on the changing doctrines of the Watchtower Society.

Key Bible verses have been mistranslated to support Watchtower theology. For the purpose of illustration, let us consider how the Watchtower Society renders three key verses—Colossians 1:16,17; John 1:1; and Titus 2:13.

Colossians 1:16,17

> For by him all things were created: things in heaven and on earth, visible and invisible, whether thrones or powers or rulers or authorities; all things were created by him and for him. He is before all things, and in him all things hold together.

The Jehovah's Witnesses mistranslate this verse in such a way to make it appear that Christ was created *first* by the Father, and then Christ was used by the Father to create *all other* things in the universe. The New World Translation reads, "By means of him all [other] things were created in the heavens and upon the earth, the things visible and the things invisible, no matter whether they are thrones or lordships or governments or authorities. All [other] things have been created through him and for him. Also, he is before all [other] things and by means of him all [other] things were made to exist"[13] (brackets appear in NWT).

There is no justification from the Greek texts for inserting the word "other" into Colossians 1:16,17 four times. The NWT is a translation with a bias, the goal being to enforce the unorthodox Watchtower Society doctrine that Jesus is a created being and is therefore not God Almighty. The fact is, Colossians 1:16 teaches that Christ created "*all* things." This being so, Christ cannot be a created being.

When speaking with a Jehovah's Witness about Colossians 1:16,17, point out that the Watchtower Society's Greek interlinear version of the Bible shows that the Greek word *panta* means "all" things and not "all other" things.

In the foreword of the New World Translation it is claimed that some words are inserted (with brackets) to make for smoother reading in the English, without changing the meaning of the text. However, the insertion of the word "other" in Colossians 1:16,17 *entirely changes the meaning of the text*.[14] The intent of the Watchtower Society is clear: to enforce the idea that Jesus is a created being and is, therefore, not God Almighty. The 1950 version of the New World Translation did not even put brackets around the four insertions of "other" in these verses.[15] This made it appear as if the word was translated from original Greek texts. Brackets were eventually inserted in the 1961 edition when evangelical scholars exposed this perversion of the text of Scripture.[16]

 A good cross-reference to share with the Jehovah's Witness is Isaiah 44:24, where God Himself asserts: "I, the LORD [Yahweh], am the maker of *all things*, stretching out the heavens *by Myself*, and spreading out the earth *all alone*" (NASB, emphasis added). If Yahweh made all things "by Myself" and did so "all alone," this obviously rules out the idea that Yahweh created Jesus first and then created everything else *through* Him. If Yahweh is called the sole creator of the universe (Isaiah 44:24) and if Jesus is called the creator of the universe (John 1:3; Colossians 1:16), then clearly this points to Jesus' identity as God.

John 1:1

> In the beginning was the Word, and the Word was with God, and the Word was God.

The Jehovah's Witnesses' New World Translation renders the last part of this verse, "The Word [Christ] was a god." Witnesses believe that because there is no definite article ("the") in the Greek in reference to Christ, it must be that Christ is "a"

God, not "the" God like the Father is.[17] Hence, they believe that the Greek text of John 1:1 is saying that Jesus was not God Almighty but rather was *godlike, divine, a god.*[18]

The NWT translation of this is incorrect for many reasons. First, the full deity of Christ is supported by many other references in John as well as the rest of the New Testament (see John 8:58; 10:30; 20:28; Colossians 1:15,16; 2:9; Titus 2:13; Hebrews 1:8). That Jesus is Jehovah (Yahweh) is clear from the fact that the New Testament consistently applies to Jesus passages and attributes that in the Old Testament apply *only* to Jehovah:

- Jesus is the great "I AM" of the Old Testament (John 8:58; compare with Exodus 3:14).

- Jesus as Yahweh was "pierced" on the cross (Revelation 1:7; compare with Zechariah 12:10).

- Yahweh's glory and Jesus' glory are equated (Isaiah 6:1-5; compare with John 12:41).

- Jesus' identity as Yahweh is proved in His role in creation (Colossians 1:16; compare with Isaiah 44:24).

- Both Yahweh and Jesus are described as having a voice like the roar of rushing waters (Ezekiel 43:2; compare with Revelation 1:15).

Further, linguists have long pointed out that it is not necessary to translate Greek nouns that have no definite article with an *indefinite* article (there is no indefinite article in Greek). In other words, the noun *theos* (Greek for "God") without the definite article *ho* (the Greek word for "the") does not need to be translated as "a God" as the Jehovah's Witnesses have done in reference to Christ. It is significant that *theos* without the definite article *ho* is used of the Father in the New Testament (Luke 20:38). Because the lack of the definite article in Luke 20:38 in reference to the Father does not mean He is a lesser God, neither does the lack of the definite article in John 1:1 in reference to Jesus mean He is a lesser God. The presence or absence of the definite article does not alter the fundamental meaning of *theos* (God).

Jesus Is "the God"

Contrary to the claims of the Watchtower Society, there are some New Testament texts that *do* use the definite article and speak of Christ as "the God" *(ho theos)*. One example is John 20:28, where Thomas says to Jesus, "My Lord and my God." The verse reads literally from the Greek: "The Lord of me and the God *[ho theos]* of me" (see also Matthew 1:23 and Hebrews 1:8). So it does not matter whether John did or did not use the definite article in John 1:1. *The Bible clearly teaches that Jesus is God,* not just a god.

Biblical scholars have noted that if John had intended an adjectival sense *(godlike or divine—a god),* he had an adjective *(theios)* ready at hand that he could have used. Instead, John says the Word *is* God *(theos)!* John was clearly saying that Jesus was (is) absolute deity. Make this clear to your Jehovah's Witness friend.

In view of such errors, it is no wonder Greek scholar Julius Mantey says of the Jehovah's Witnesses' translation of John 1:1: "Ninety-nine percent of the scholars of the world who know Greek and who have helped translate the Bible are in disagreement with the Jehovah's Witnesses."[19]

Titus 2:13

The Jehovah's Witnesses translate this verse, "While we wait for the happy hope and glorious manifestation of the great God and of [the] Savior of us, Christ Jesus" (brackets in original). This translation makes it appear that *two* persons are in view—the "great God" (the Father) and the "Savior" (Jesus Christ).[20] This is in contrast to, for example, the New American Standard Bible, which renders this verse: "Looking for the blessed hope and the appearing of the glory of our great God *and* Savior, Christ Jesus" (emphasis added).

Greek grammarians say that when there are two nouns that are the same case connected with the word "and" (Greek: *kai),* and the first noun is preceded by the definite article ("the") while the second noun *is not* preceded by the definite article, then the second noun refers to the identical person or thing the first noun refers to. This is the case in Titus 2:13. Two nouns, "God" and "Savior," are joined together with "and." The definite article precedes the first noun ("God") but not the second noun ("Savior"). The sentence literally reads: "The great God and Savior of us." The two nouns in question, "God" and "Savior," are referring to the same person—Jesus Christ.

 Point out to the Jehovah's Witness that the teaching in Titus 2:13 that Jesus is God *and* Savior is consistent with other Scripture verses. In Isaiah 43:11, God asserts: "I, even I, am the LORD [Yahweh], and apart from me there is no savior." This verse indicates that 1) a claim to be Savior is a claim to deity, and 2) there is only one Savior—God. It is against this backdrop that the New Testament refers to Jesus as Savior (Luke 2:11). The parallel truths that *only* God is the Savior (Isaiah 43:11) and that Jesus *is* the Savior constitute powerful evidence for Christ's deity.

The New World Translation is inaccurate and misleading.

✓ Biblical linguists give a universal "thumbs down" to the NWT.

✓ The translators of the NWT were not true biblical linguists.

✓ The NWT has gone through major changes through the years.

✓ The NWT has consistently mistranslated key Bible verses to support deviant Watchtower theology.

For further information on the inaccuracy of the New World Translation, consult *Reasoning from the Scriptures with the Jehovah's Witnesses,* pp. 71-120.

3

God Has Other Names
Besides Jehovah

Jehovah's Witnesses are told through Watchtower Society (WS) publications that God's true name is Jehovah. They are taught that superstitious Jewish scribes long ago removed this sacred name from the Bible. But there is no need to worry, the Watchtower says. In the New World Translation of the Holy Scriptures the Watchtower Society has "faithfully" restored the divine name in the Old Testament where the Hebrew consonants "YHWH" appear.[1]

Moreover, as noted in the previous chapter, the Watchtower New World Bible Translation Committee has inserted the name Jehovah in the New Testament in verses where the text is believed to refer to the Father.[2] The WS has taken the liberty to do this despite the fact that it goes against the thousands of Greek manuscripts of the New Testament that have been discovered—some of which date from the second century.

When a Jehovah's Witness shows up on your doorstep, he or she will often point to the importance of using God's correct name, Jehovah. The Witness will typically open up the New World Translation (NWT) and cite Exodus 3:15 to the effect that Jehovah is God's name "to time indefinite." They also cite

Romans 10:13 (NWT): "Everyone who calls on the name of Jehovah will be saved." In citing passages like this, the Jehovah's Witness often convinces the unwary and biblically illiterate person that the proper use of God's "correct" name (Jehovah) is essential to his or her salvation.

Watchtower Society's View of God's Name

- God's only true name is Jehovah.
- Use of God's correct name is essential to salvation.

The biblical evidence shows the Watchtower Society's viewpoint on God's name is untenable. The evidence indicates that 1) the word "Jehovah" is a manmade term; 2) "Jehovah" or "Yahweh" is not the only name by which God is known; 3) Jesus *never* referred to the Father as "Jehovah" in the New Testament; 4) believers are uniquely privileged to call God "Father"; 5) salvation *does not* depend upon adherence to the name "Jehovah"; and 6) the New Testament consistently uplifts Jesus.

"Jehovah" is a manmade term. This name is not found in the Hebrew and Greek manuscripts from which English translations of the Bible are derived.[3] The Old Testament does contain the name *Yahweh*—or, more literally, YHWH (the original Hebrew had only consonants).

Where did the word "Jehovah" come from? The ancient Jews had a superstitious dread of pronouncing the name *Yhwh*. They felt that if they uttered this name, they might violate the Third Commandment, which deals with taking God's name in vain (Exodus 20:7). To avoid the possibility of breaking this commandment, the Jews for centuries substituted the name *Adonai*

(Lord) or some other name in its place whenever they came across it in public readings of Scripture.

Eventually, the fearful Hebrew scribes decided to insert the vowels from Adonai (a-o-a) within the consonants, YHWH.[4] The result was *Yahowah*, or Jehovah. The word "Jehovah" is derived from a consonant–vowel combination from the words "YHWH" and "Adonai." Watchtower literature acknowledges this fact.[5]

The point, then, is that Jehovah is not a biblical term. Of course, there are other translations besides the NWT that have used the term "Jehovah." The American Standard Version (1901) consistently uses the term. The King James Version uses the term in four instances (Exodus 6:3; Psalm 83:18; Isaiah 12:2; 26:4).[6] The New English Bible also uses the term in Exodus 3:15 and 6:3. Jehovah's Witnesses often impress people by pointing to such verses where the name "Jehovah" is used in these translations. It gives the appearance that the Witnesses are correct in saying that God's true name is Jehovah.

We must be careful to note that though there is no biblical justification for the term "Jehovah," scholars are not precisely clear as to the correct way to pronounce the Hebrew word YHWH.[7] Though most modern scholars believe Yahweh is the correct rendering (as I do), we really cannot criticize the Jehovah's Witnesses for using this term when the Hebrew consonants YHWH appear in the Old Testament. After all, some evangelical Christians and some legitimate Bible translations (in the Old Testament) use "Jehovah" as well. (However, Jehovah's Witnesses *can* be criticized and proven wrong regarding the insertion of this name in the New Testament.)

Because many people have accepted the term "Jehovah" as the conventional way of referring to God, the primary point of contention with the Jehovah's Witnesses must not be the term itself, but rather *how they use this term* in their biblical interpretation and theology.

"Jehovah" or "Yahweh" is not the only name by which God is known. Contrary to the claims of Jehovah's Witnesses, God is identified in other ways in Scripture besides the name Jehovah. One example of this is the expression *the God of Abraham, God of Isaac, and God of Jacob* which occurs many times in Scripture.[8] Though God is definitely known by the name Jehovah (or, more properly, Yahweh), He is not known *only* by the name Jehovah (or Yahweh).

God is also called *El Shaddai* (Genesis 17:1-20). "El" in Hebrew refers to "Mighty God." But "Shaddai" qualifies this meaning and adds something to it. Many scholars believe "Shaddai" is derived from a root word that refers to a mother's breast. This name, then, indicates not only that God is a Mighty God, but that He is full of compassion, grace, and mercy.

 Point out to the Jehovah's Witness that God is called the *Lord of Hosts* in the Bible. This title pictures God as the sovereign commander of a great heavenly army of angels (Psalm 89:6,8). Further, God is called our *rock* (Deuteronomy 32:4-31). This points to God's strength and power. God is called our *fortress* (Psalm 18:2). This speaks of the protection God provides us. God is called our *shield* (Genesis 15:1). This points to God as our daily defense. God is also called our *strength* (1 Samuel 15:29 KJV). This points to how God infuses us with His power so we can face any circumstance. The point is, there are *many* different names and ascriptions used for God in the Bible.

 Jesus never referred to God the Father as "Jehovah." If the Jehovah's Witnesses are correct that God must always be called by the name Jehovah, then Jesus was way out of line, for He *never* used this name when referring to the Father. (Even though the New World Translation sometimes puts the word "Jehovah" in Jesus' mouth in the New Testament, the reality is that the word Jehovah *does not occur a single time* in any legitimate manuscript copy of the New Testament.)

Encourage the Jehovah's Witness to consider the "Lord's Prayer." Jesus did not begin this prayer with the words, "Jehovah God in heaven." Rather, He said, "Our Father in heaven" (Matthew 6:9).[9] (The NWT renders it, "Our Father in the heavens.") Jesus began other prayers with "Father" as well (see Matthew 11:25; 26:39-42; Mark 14:36; Luke 10:21; 22:42; 23:34).[10] Help your friend see that "Jehovah" is not the only name or ascription by which God is known.

Believers are uniquely privileged to call God "Father." Because we are God's children, we are uniquely privileged to come before the Father and call out to him, "Abba, Father!" (Romans 8:15; Galatians 4:6). The fact that we can address God with the more intimate term "Father" proves we are not to woodenly interpret Exodus 3:15 as meaning that Jehovah is the only expression by which God can be addressed "to time indefinite."[11] In context, the main point of Exodus 3:15 is that people of all generations would come to understand *who God is* in His true nature and being; He is eternally self-existent and the sovereign Lord of the universe. This is what the word "Jehovah" reveals about God.

Salvation does not depend upon adherence to the name "Jehovah." As noted earlier, the New World Translation renders Romans 10:13, "Everyone who calls on the name of Jehovah will be saved." In citing this passage (and others like it), Jehovah's Witnesses say the proper use of God's "correct" name, Jehovah, is essential to salvation.

In reality, the NWT mistranslates this verse. The original Greek has no reference to "Jehovah." This word was inserted into the text by the Watchtower Society's translators. The New International Version correctly translates this verse as: "Everyone who calls on the name *of the Lord* [Greek: *kurios*] will be saved" (emphasis added). In the broader context of Romans 13:9-13, it is clear that "Lord" in verse 13 is referring to Jesus Christ. (See verse 9, where Jesus is *explicitly identified* as the "Lord" of these five verses.)[12]

Romans 10:13 is actually a quote from Joel 2:32: "And everyone who calls on the name of the LORD [Yahweh] will be saved." This doesn't give justification for using the word "Yahweh" or "Jehovah" in Romans 10:13. As noted previously, the word used in the Greek manuscripts for "Lord" is *kurios*, not *Yahweh*. But here is what is significant about Joel 2:32: As much as the Jehovah's Witness may want to deny it, the apostle Paul is quoting Joel 2:32 ("calling upon *Yahweh*") in the context of *being fulfilled* by calling upon *Jesus Christ* for salvation. "Calling upon Yahweh" and "calling upon Jesus" are equated. This is clear evidence pointing to Christ's identity as Yahweh.

Calling on "the Lord"

Like Paul, Peter quotes from Joel 2:32 when preaching on the day of Pentecost: "And it shall be that everyone who calls on the name of the Lord will be saved" (Acts 2:21 NASB). Verses 22-36 prove that the "Lord" Peter is speaking of is Jesus. This "Lord" was attested by miracles and wonders on earth, was nailed to a cross, was raised from the dead, and ascended to the right hand of the Father!

The New Testament consistently uplifts Jesus. It seems clear that the Watchtower Society's insertion of "Jehovah" throughout the New Testament is an attempt to cloud the truth—that the name the New Testament consistently uplifts is Jesus, *not* Jehovah.

 My apologetics colleague Marian Bodine suggests key questions you can ask a Jehovah's Witness to demonstrate that the New Testament uplifts Jesus:

- In whose name should we meet together (Matthew 18:20; 1 Corinthians 5:4)?

- Demons are subject to whose name (Luke 10:17; Acts 16:18)?

- Repentance and forgiveness should be preached in whose name (Luke 24:47)?

- In whose name are you to believe and receive the forgiveness of sins (John 1:12; 3:16; Acts 10:43; 1 John 3:23; 5:13)?

- By whose name, and no other, do we obtain salvation (Acts 4:12)?

- Whose name should be invoked as we bring our petitions to God in prayer (John 14:13, 14; 15:16; 16:23,24)?

- In whose name is the Holy Spirit sent (John 14:26)?

- Whose name and authority was invoked by the disciples in healing the sick and lame (Acts 3:16; 4:7-10,30)?

- Whose name did Paul tell us to call upon (1 Corinthians 1:2)?

- Whose name is above every name (Ephesians 1:20,21; Philippians 2:9-11)?[13]

The answer to each of these questions is *Jesus,* and this should get the attention of any fair-minded Jehovah's Witness. The Scripture references mentioned should be more than adequate to demonstrate the name by which *true* followers of God should be identified.

God Has Other Names Besides Jehovah

✓ The word "Jehovah" is a manmade term.

✓ Jehovah, or Yahweh, is not the only name by which God is known.

✓ Jesus never referred to God the Father as Jehovah in the New Testament.

✓ Believers are uniquely privileged to call God "Father."

✓ Salvation does not depend upon adherence to using the name Jehovah.

✓ The New Testament consistently uplifts Jesus.

For further information on the Watchtower's position on the divine name, consult *Reasoning from the Scriptures with the Jehovah's Witnesses,* pp. 49-69.

4

Jesus Is
God Almighty

Jehovah's Witnesses say Jesus was created as the archangel Michael billions of years ago. Michael (Jesus) was allegedly created first, and then he was used by God to create all other things in the universe (see Colossians 1:16 NWT).

Jehovah's Witnesses concede that Jesus is a "mighty god," but deny He is God Almighty. To support this claim, they point to passages that seem to indicate Jesus is inferior to the Father. For example, Jesus said "the Father is greater than I" (John 14:28) and referred to the Father as "my God" (John 20:17). First Corinthians 11:3 tells us that "the head of Christ is God." Jesus is called God's "only begotten son" (John 3:16 NASB) and the "firstborn over all creation" (Colossians 1:15). Jehovah's Witnesses thus reason that Jesus is not God in the same sense Jehovah is and should not be worshiped.

Though Michael (Jesus) existed in his prehuman state for billions of years, at the appointed time he was born on earth as a human being, ceasing his existence as an angel. In order to "ransom" humankind from sin, Michael gave up his existence as a spirit creature (angel) when his life force was transferred into Mary's womb by Jehovah. This was not an incarnation (God in the flesh). Rather, Jesus became a perfect human. He also died as a human.

41

According to the Watchtower Society, Jesus was crucified on a stake. They say the cross is a pagan religious symbol the church adopted when Satan took control of ecclesiastical authority in the early centuries of Christianity.[1]

When Jesus died, He became nonexistent and was raised *(recreated)* three days later as a spirit creature (that is, as Michael the Archangel). A physical resurrection did not occur. Jesus gave up His human life as a ransom sacrifice for the benefit of humankind. "Having given up his flesh for the life of the world, Christ could never take it again and become a man once more."[2]

In terms of how Jesus *proved* His "resurrection" to the disciples, Witnesses say He "appeared to His disciples on different occasions in various fleshly bodies, just as angels had appeared to men of ancient times. Like those angels, he had the power to construct and to disintegrate those fleshly bodies at will, for the purpose of proving visibly that he had been resurrected."[3]

Consistent with Jesus' alleged spiritual resurrection is the teaching that a spiritual "second coming" of Christ occurred in 1914. According to Jehovah's Witnesses, He has since been ruling as King on earth through the Watchtower Society.

Watchtower Society's View of Christ

- Jesus was created by the Father as the Archangel Michael billions of years ago.

- Jesus is a mighty god, but not God Almighty like the Father.

- Jesus was later born on earth as a mere human.

- Jesus was crucified on a stake, not a cross.

- Following His death, Jesus *spiritually* resurrected from the dead.

- The spiritual Second Coming of Christ occurred in 1914.

The Bible proves Jesus is God Almighty. Scripture provides ample evidence that 1) Jesus *was not* created as Michael the Archangel; 2) Jesus *is not* a lesser god than God the Father; 3) Jesus *was (is)* Yahweh; 4) the incarnate Christ *was* God in human flesh; 5) Jesus *was physically resurrected* from the dead; and 6) the Second Coming *will be* bodily and visible.

Jesus was not created as Michael the Archangel. Michael, in Daniel 10:13, is called "one of the chief princes." The fact that he is "one of" the chief princes indicates that he is part of a group of chief princes. How large that group is, we are not told. But the fact that Michael is one among equals proves he is not unique. By contrast, the Greek word used to describe Jesus in John 3:16 ("God's one and only Son") is *monogenes*—meaning "unique" or "one of a kind." He is not a "chief prince." He is the unique "King of kings and Lord of lords" (Revelation 19:16).

Jesus Created the Angels

Colossians 1:16 says of Jesus, "For by him all things were created: things in heaven and on earth, visible and invisible, whether thrones or powers or rulers or authorities; all things were created by him and for him." "Thrones," "powers," "rulers," and "authorities" were Jewish words used to describe angels. Jesus was not an angel; He was the *creator* of angels.

Moreover, in Hebrews 1:5 we are told that no angel can ever be called God's son: "To which of the angels did God ever say, 'You are my Son...'" Since Jesus is the Son of God, and since no angel can ever be called God's son, then Jesus cannot possibly be the Archangel Michael.

Further, we are told in Hebrews 2:5 that the world is not (and will not be) in subjection to an angel. The backdrop to this is that the Dead Sea Scrolls (discovered at Qumran in 1947) reflect an expectation that the Archangel Michael would be a supreme figure in the coming messianic kingdom. It may be that some of the recipients of the book of Hebrews were tempted to assign angels a place above Christ. Hebrews 2:5 makes it clear that *no* angel will rule in God's kingdom. This being so, Christ cannot be Michael since He is repeatedly said to be the ruler of God's kingdom in Scripture (Genesis 49:10; 2 Samuel 7:16; Psalm 2:6; Daniel 7:13,14; Luke 1:32,33; Matthew 2:1,2; Revelation 19:16).

Point out to the Jehovah's Witness that the Archangel Michael does not have the authority in himself to rebuke Satan. In Jude 9 (NASB) we read, "But Michael the archangel, when he disputed with the devil and argued about the body of Moses, did not dare pronounce against him a railing judgment, but said, 'The Lord rebuke you.'" By contrast, Jesus rebuked the devil on a number of occasions (for example, Matthew 4:10). Since Michael could not rebuke the devil in his own authority and Jesus could *(and did)*, Michael and Jesus cannot be the same person. (In fact, Jesus is "the Lord" Michael appealed to when he said "the Lord rebuke you....")

Jesus is not a lesser God than the Father. Though Jehovah's Witnesses cite a barrage of biblical verses to "prove" Jesus is a lesser God than the Father, in each case they misinterpret the passage in question.

Isaiah 9:6

> For to us a child is born, to us a son is given, and the government will be on his shoulders. And he will be called Wonderful Counselor, Mighty God, Everlasting Father, Prince of Peace.

Because this messianic verse refers to Jesus as "Mighty God," Jehovah's Witnesses reason that Jesus is a lesser God than the Father because the Father is referred to as God *Almighty*. However, in Isaiah 10:21, Yahweh (Jehovah) is called "Mighty God" (using the same Hebrew word *Elohim*). This obliterates any suggestion that the expression must refer to a lesser deity. The Father and Jesus are equally divine.

Mark 13:32

> [Jesus said,] "No one knows about that day or hour, not even the angels in heaven, nor the Son, but only the Father."

Jehovah's Witnesses reason that since Jesus does not know the hour of His return, He must be lesser than God the Father who is omniscient. This allegation is easily answered. Christ as God *is* omniscient (see Matthew 11:27; 17:27; Luke 5:4,6; John 7:29; 8:55; 10:15; 16:30; 17:25; 21:6-11; 21:17), but in the incarnation He took on a human nature, which *is not* omniscient. *It was only from His humanity* that Christ could say He did not know the day or hour of His return. Philippians 2:5-11 indicates that Christ—in order to fulfill His messianic role on earth—*voluntarily* chose not to use some of His divine attributes (like omniscience) on some occasions.

John 3:16

> For God so loved the world, that He gave His only begotten Son, that whoever believes in Him shall not perish, but have eternal life (NASB).

Jehovah's Witnesses reason that because Jesus is called God's "only begotten Son," He must not be God in the sense that the Father is. However, the phrase "only begotten" (Greek: *monogenes*) does not mean Christ was *created*. It means "unique" or "one of a kind." Jesus is the "Son of God" in that He uniquely has the same nature as the Father—a *divine* nature (see John 5:18).

The fact that Christ was called "Son of God" is an indication of His full deity. Though the term "son of" can refer to "offspring of," it carries the more important meaning "of the order of." The phrase is often used this way in the Old Testament: "Sons of the prophets" meant "of the order of prophets" (1 Kings 20:35). "Sons of the singers" meant "of the order of singers" (Nehemiah 12:28 NASB). Likewise, "Son of God" means "of the order of God" and represents a claim to undiminished deity.

Jesus the Son

The ancients often used the phrase "Son of..." to indicate *equality of being*. When Jesus claimed to be the Son of God, His Jewish contemporaries understood He was claiming to be God. They insisted, "We have a law, and according to that law he [Christ] must die, because he claimed to be the Son of God" (John 19:7; see also 5:18). Recognizing Jesus was identifying Himself as God, the Jews wanted to kill Him for committing blasphemy.

Clear evidence for Christ's *eternal* Sonship is found in the fact that Christ is represented as *already being the Son of God* before His birth in Bethlehem. For instance, recall Jesus' discussion with Nicodemus in John 3. Jesus said, "For God so loved the world that he gave his one and only Son, that whoever believes in him shall not perish but have eternal life. For God did not send his Son *into* the world to condemn the world, but to save the world through him" (verses 16,17, emphasis added).

That Christ—as the Son of God—was *sent into* the world implies that He was the Son of God before the Incarnation.

 Hebrews 1:2 says God created the universe *through* His "Son," implying that Christ was the Son of God *prior* to the Creation. Moreover, Christ as the Son is explicitly said to have existed "before all things" (Colossians 1:17; compare with verses 13,14). As well, Jesus, speaking as the Son of God (John 8:54-56), asserts His eternal preexistence before Abraham (verse 58).

John 14:28

> ...[Jesus said,] If you loved me, you would be glad that I am going to the Father, for the Father is greater than I.

Jehovah's Witnesses reason that since the Father is "greater" than Jesus, Jesus must be a lesser God than the Father. However, in this verse Jesus is not speaking about His nature (Christ had earlier said "I and the Father are one" in this regard—see John 10:30), but is rather speaking of His lowly position in the Incarnation. The Father was seated upon the throne of highest majesty in heaven. It was far different with His incarnate Son who was despised and rejected, surrounded by implacable enemies, and soon to be nailed to a criminal's cross. From His low position on earth, Jesus could honestly say that the Father was "greater" than Him.

First Corinthians 11:3

> ...The head of every man is Christ, and the head of the woman is man, and the head of Christ is God.

Because 1 Corinthians 11:3 says "the head of Christ is God," Jehovah's Witnesses reason that Jesus must be a lesser deity than the Father. Notice, however, that Paul says in this same verse that the man is the head of the woman, even though men and women are *equal* in their essential nature (Genesis 1:26-28). This indicates that *equality of being* and *functional subordination* are not mutually exclusive. Christ and the Father are equal in nature (John 10:30), though Jesus is functionally under the Father's headship.

Colossians 1:15

> He is the image of the invisible God, the firstborn over all creation.

Jehovah's Witnesses reason that since Jesus is called "firstborn," He must have come into being at a point in time and is, therefore, a lesser God than the Father. However, "firstborn" (Greek: *prototokos*) does not mean "first-created," but rather "first in rank, preeminent one, heir."[4] [Though King David was actually the last son born to Jesse, he was called "firstborn" because he became the preeminent son (Psalm 89:27).] Christ is the "firstborn of creation" in the sense that He is *positionally* preeminent over creation and is supreme over all things.

For Colossians 1:15 to mean "first created," Paul would not have called Christ the "firstborn" *(prototokos)* but the "first-created" *(protoktisis)*—a term that is *never* used of Christ in the New Testament. That Christ is preeminent over creation makes sense since He is the Creator of creation (see verse 16). Emphasize this fact to your Jehovah's Witness friend.

Jesus was (is) Yahweh. A comparison of the Old and New Testaments provides powerful testimony to Jesus' identity as Yahweh. In Isaiah 43:11, for example, Yahweh asserts: "I, even I, am the LORD, and *apart from me there is no savior*" (emphasis added). This verse indicates that 1) a claim to be Savior is, in itself, a claim to deity; and 2) there is only one Savior—God (Yahweh). Against this backdrop, it is truly revealing of Christ's divine nature that the New Testament refers to Him as the Savior (Luke 2:11; John 4:42).

Another key passage is Isaiah 6:1-5, where the prophet recounts his vision of Yahweh "seated on a throne, high and exalted" (verse 1). He said, "Holy, holy, holy is the LORD *[Yahweh]* Almighty; the whole earth is full of his glory" (verse 3). Isaiah also quotes Yahweh as saying: "I am the LORD; that is my name! I will not give my glory to another" (42:8). Later, the apostle John under the inspiration of the Holy Spirit wrote that Isaiah actually "saw Jesus' glory" (John 12:41). Yahweh's glory and Jesus' glory are equated.

Further support is found in Christ's crucifixion. In Zechariah 12:10, Yahweh is speaking prophetically: "They will look on me, the one they have pierced." Though Yahweh is speaking, this is obviously a reference to Christ's future crucifixion. We know that "the one they have pierced" is Jesus, for He is described this same way by the apostle John in Revelation 1:7.

In Isaiah 40:3 we read a prophecy of John the Baptist preparing the way for Jesus: "A voice of one calling: 'In the desert prepare the way for the LORD *[Yahweh]*; make straight in the wilderness a highway for our God *[Elohim].*'" That this verse was written in reference to the future ministry of Christ is clear in John 1:23, where John refers to Isaiah 40:3. This means that within the context of a single verse, Christ is called both Yahweh and Elohim.

Moreover, contrary to Jehovah's Witnesses, Christ *was* truly worshiped as God many times according to the Gospel accounts. He accepted worship from Thomas (John 20:28), the angels (Hebrews 1:6), some wise men (Matthew 2:11), a leper (Matthew 8:2), a ruler (Matthew 9:18), a blind man (John 9:38), "Mary Magdalene and the other Mary" (Matthew 28:9), and the disciples (Matthew 28:17). The fact that Jesus willingly received worship on various occasions says a lot about His true identity, for Scripture reveals that *only God* (Yahweh) can be worshiped (Exodus 34:14).

A Few Key Questions

- If it is *only God* who can save, and if there is *no other Savior* than God (Isaiah 43:11), then doesn't this mean that New Testament references to Jesus *as Savior* point to His deity (Titus 2:13)?

- If the same Greek word used for worshiping the Father is used of worshiping Jesus *(proskuneo)*, why does the Watchtower Society deny Jesus should be worshiped?

- In Isaiah 40:3, did you know the word "Lord" is *Yahweh* and the word "God" is *Elohim?* Consider the verse: "In the desert prepare the way for the LORD *[Yahweh]*; make straight in the wilderness a highway for our God *[Elohim]*." Since John 1:23 indicates that these words were fulfilled in John the Baptist preparing the way *for Jesus*, is it not clear that Jesus is called Yahweh and Elohim by Isaiah?

The Incarnate Christ was God in human flesh. Contrary to the Watchtower view that Jesus during the incarnate state was *just* a man and nothing more, we must ask, "Why send Jesus at all?"[5] After all, since according to Jehovah's Witnesses all that was required for sacrifice was "a perfect human," God could easily have created one from scratch if He wanted. There was certainly no need for God to send His Son.

Scripture provides plenty of evidence that in the incarnation Jesus was *truly God in human flesh*. Colossians 2:9, for example, tells us, "For in Christ all the fullness of the Deity lives in bodily form." Jesus thus fulfilled the prophecy found in Isaiah 7:14:

" 'The virgin will be with child and will give birth to a son, and they will call him Immanuel'—which means, 'God with us' " (Matthew 1:23). Jesus, born as a human, was literally "God with us."

 Jesus was a perfect redeemer precisely because He is both God *and* man. If Christ had been *only* God, He could not have died since God, by His very nature, cannot die. It was only as a man that Christ could represent humanity and die. As God, however, Christ's death had infinite value sufficient to provide redemption for the sins of all humankind. Clearly, then, Christ had to be both God *and* man to secure our salvation (1 Timothy 2:5; see also Hebrews 2:14-16).

 Jesus physically resurrected. The resurrected Jesus asserted to the disciples, "Look at my hands and my feet. It is I myself! Touch me and see; a ghost does not have flesh and bones, as you see I have" (Luke 24:39). Notice three things here: 1) the resurrected Christ indicates in this verse that He is not a spirit; 2) the resurrected Christ indicates that His resurrection body is made up of flesh and bones; and 3) Christ's physical hands and feet represent physical proof of His resurrection from the dead.

Further support for the physical resurrection of Christ can be found in Christ's words recorded in John 2:19-21: "Jesus answered them, 'Destroy this temple, and I will raise it again in three days.' The Jews replied, 'It has taken forty-six years to build this temple, and you are going to raise it in three days?' But the temple he had spoken of was his body." Jesus was saying He would be *bodily* raised from the dead, not raised as a spirit creature.

The resurrected Christ ate physical food on four different occasions. He did this as a means of proving He had a real physical body (Luke 24:30,42,43; John 21:12,13; Acts 1:4). It would have been deception on Jesus' part to have offered His ability to eat physical food as a proof of His bodily resurrection if He had not been resurrected in a physical body.

 The physical body of the resurrected Christ was touched by different people. He was touched by Mary (John 20:17) and other women (Matthew 28:9). He challenged the disciples to physically touch Him so they could rest assured that His body was material in nature (Luke 24:39). This is in keeping with the scriptural fact that the body that is "sown" in death is the very same body that is *raised in life* (1 Corinthians 15:35-44). That which goes into the grave is raised to life (see verse 42). Clearly, Christ physically resurrected from the dead.

The Second Coming will be bodily and visible. One Greek word used to describe the Second Coming in 1 Peter 4:13 is *apokalupsis*, which carries the basic meaning of "revelation," "visible disclosure," "unveiling," and "removing the cover" from something that is hidden. Christ's Second Coming will be a visible event.

Another Greek word used of Christ's Second Coming is *epiphaneia*, which carries the basic meaning of "to appear." This word literally means "a shining forth." It is used several times by the apostle Paul in reference to Christ's visible Second Coming. For example, in Titus 2:13 (NASB), Paul speaks of "looking for the blessed hope and the appearing of the glory of our great God and Savior, Christ Jesus." In 1 Timothy 6:14 (NASB), Paul urges Timothy to "keep the commandment without stain or reproach until the appearing of our Lord Jesus Christ." Significantly, Christ's first coming or "appearing," which was both bodily and visible, was called an *epiphaneia* (2 Timothy 1:10). In the same way, Christ's Second Coming will be bodily and visible.

Matthew supports the visible coming of the Lord: "Immediately after the distress of those days 'the sun will be darkened, and the moon will not give its light; the stars will fall from the sky, and the heavenly bodies will be shaken.' At that time the sign of the Son of Man will appear in the sky, and all the nations of the earth will mourn. They will see the Son of Man coming on the clouds of the sky, with power and great glory" (Matthew 24:29,30).

Be aware that Jehovah's Witnesses sometimes argue that Acts 1:9-11 proves that Jesus will return *invisibly:* "After he said this, he was taken up before their very eyes, and a cloud hid him from their sight. They were looking intently up into the sky as he was going, when suddenly two men dressed in white stood beside them. 'Men of Galilee,' they said, 'why do you stand here looking into the sky? This same Jesus, who has been taken from you into heaven, will come back in the same way you have seen him go into heaven.'" Witnesses argue that the "manner" of Jesus' ascent was that He *disappeared from view*, and His departure was observed only by His disciples. The world was not aware of what had happened. This passage allegedly indicates that the same would be true of Christ's Second Coming—that is, the world would be unaware of Christ's invisible coming.[6] And, indeed, the world was largely unaware of Christ's alleged coming in 1914.

The Watchtower Society is confusing "manner" with "result." The *manner* of Jesus' ascent was not "disappearing from view"; rather, the *result* of Jesus' ascent was "disappearing from view." The actual manner of Jesus' ascent was *visible* and *bodily*. Jesus visibly and bodily ascended, with the result of disappearing from view when He passed through the clouds. Likewise, at the

Second Coming, Christ will come visibly and bodily and will *appear* into view.

Jesus Is God Almighty

✓ Scripture distinguishes between Michael the Archangel (a creature) and Jesus (the Creator).

✓ Scriptures cited by Witnesses to prove Jesus is a lesser god are taken out of context.

✓ Scripture proves that Jesus was (is) Yahweh.

✓ Jesus *physically* resurrected from the dead.

✓ Jesus will physically and visibly return at His Second Coming.

For further information on refuting the Watchtower view of Jesus Christ, consult *Reasoning from the Scriptures with the Jehovah's Witnesses*, pp. 71-194.

5

The Holy Spirit
Is God,
Not a "Force"

In Watchtower Society (WS) theology, the Holy Spirit is neither a person nor God. Rather, the Holy Spirit is God's impersonal "active force" for accomplishing His will in the world. WS literature likens the Holy Spirit to electricity: "a force that can be adapted to perform a great variety of operations."[1] It was this force of God that allegedly came upon Jesus in the form of a dove at His baptism—a dynamic power that enabled Him to perform many miracles (Mark 1:10).

In proof of the WS position, it is argued that Scripture portrays many people being "filled" by the Holy Spirit. Such an expression would be appropriate, we are told, *only* if the Holy Spirit were a force and not a person.[2] After all, how can one person "fill" thousands of people at the same time? A person cannot be split up that way.

Besides, if the Holy Spirit were a person, it would have a name just as the Father and the Son do. We know from Scripture, the Watchtower Society says, that the Father's personal name is Jehovah. Likewise, the Son's personal name is Jesus. But nowhere in Scripture is a personal name ascribed to the Holy Spirit.[3] Therefore, the Holy Spirit must not be a person like the Father and the Son.

Watchtower View of the Holy Spirit

- The Holy Spirit is not a person but is a "force" of God.
- Only a force could fill many people at the same time.
- The Holy Spirit, as a force, has no personal name like the Father and Jesus.

The Bible proves the Holy Spirit is both God and a person—the third person of the Trinity. Scripture indicates that 1) the Holy Spirit is God; 2) the Holy Spirit has all the attributes of personality; 3) the Holy Spirit's works confirm His personality; 4) the Holy Spirit is treated as a person; 5) the "lack of a name" argument is fallacious; and 6) the "filling many people" argument is fallacious.

The Holy Spirit is God. We know this to be true because Acts 5:3,4 indicates that lying to the Holy Spirit and lying to God are equated. Further, in 2 Corinthians 3:17,18, the Holy Spirit is called "Lord." The Holy Spirit is often identified with Yahweh (Numbers 24:2-4,12,13; Acts 7:51; 28:25-27; 1 Corinthians 2:12; Hebrews 3:7-9; 10:15-17; 2 Peter 1:21) and is spoken of as divine (Matthew 12:32; Mark 3:29; 1 Corinthians 3:16; 6:19; Ephesians 2:22). The Holy Spirit is often referred to as the "Spirit of God," thus indicating His full deity (Genesis 1:2; Exodus 31:3; 1 Samuel 10:10; 11:6; 19:23; 2 Chronicles 15:1; 24:20; Job 33:4; Ezekiel 11:24; Romans 8:9; 8:14; 1 Corinthians 2:11,14; 3:16; 6:11; 7:40; 1 Peter 4:14; 1 John 4:2).

Furthermore, the Holy Spirit has all the attributes of deity: omnipresence (Psalm 139:7), omniscience (1 Corinthians 2:10), omnipotence (Romans 15:19), holiness (John 16:7-14), and eternality (Hebrews 9:14). Since only God can have such divine attributes, it is clear the Holy Spirit is God. Also, the Holy Spirit does things only God can do: He participated in the creation of the universe (Genesis 1:2,3; Job 33:4; Psalm 104:30; Isaiah 40:12-14), begat Christ in the womb of Mary (Luke 1:35), and inspired Scripture (2 Timothy 3:16; 2 Peter 1:21).

 If the Holy Spirit is equated with God, is spoken of as divine, has all the attributes of deity, and does things only God can do, doesn't this mean the Holy Spirit is God?

 The Holy Spirit has all the attributes of personality. It has long been recognized that the three primary attributes of personality are mind, emotions, and will. A "force" does not have these attributes.

The Holy Spirit Has a Mind

The Holy Spirit's intellect is seen in 1 Corinthians 2:10 where we are told that "the Spirit searches all things" (see also Isaiah 11:2; Ephesians 1:17). (Note that the Greek word for "search" means to "thoroughly investigate a matter.") We are also told in 1 Corinthians 2:11 that the Holy Spirit "knows" the thoughts of God. How can the Spirit "know" the things of God if the Spirit does not have a mind? Thought processes require the presence of a mind.

Romans 8:27 tells us that just as the Holy Spirit knows the things of God, so God the Father "knows the mind of the Spirit." The word translated "mind" in this verse literally means "way of thinking, mind-set, aim, aspiration, striving."[4] A mere force—electricity, for example—does not think or possess a mind-set.

The Holy Spirit Has Emotions

In Ephesians 4:30 we are admonished, "Do not grieve the Holy Spirit of God." Grief is an emotion, which is not something that can be experienced by a force. *Grief is felt.* The Holy Spirit feels the emotion of grief when believers sin. In the context of Ephesians, such sins include lying, anger, stealing, laziness, and speaking unkind words (see verses 25-29).

> ### Emotions and Personality
>
> The Corinthians experienced *sorrow* after the apostle Paul wrote them a stern letter (2 Corinthians 2:2,5 NASB). The same Greek word is used in Ephesians 4:30 (translated "grieve"). Just as the Corinthian believers experienced sorrow or grief, so the Holy Spirit can experience sorrow or grief.

The Holy Spirit Has a Will

We are told in 1 Corinthians 12:11 (NASB) that the Holy Spirit distributes spiritual gifts "to each one individually just as He wills." The phrase "He wills" translates the Greek word *bouletai,* which refers to "decisions of the will after previous deliberation."[5] The Holy Spirit makes a sovereign choice regarding what spiritual gifts each Christian receives. A force does not have such a will.

Does electricity have a mind, emotions, and a will? Of course not! Electricity is just a force. But the Holy Spirit *does* have a mind, emotions, and a will, and, therefore, is a person. Be ready to support this from Scripture.

The Watchtower Society claims that this "active force" of God is sometimes *personified* in Scripture. This is not unlike other things that are personified in Scripture, such as wisdom, sin, and death. For example, Jehovah's Witnesses cite the New English Bible's rendering of Genesis 4:7: "Sin is a demon crouching at the door," personifying sin as a wicked spirit at Cain's door.[6] But, of course, "sin is not a spirit person; nor does personifying the holy spirit make it a spirit person."[7]

Aside from the arguments for the Holy Spirit's personality in this chapter, point out that the Holy Spirit used personal pronouns of Himself. An example of this is Acts 13:2: "While they were worshiping the Lord and fasting, the Holy Spirit said, 'Set apart for *me* Barnabas and Saul for the work to which *I* have called them'" (emphasis added). Regardless of what the Jehovah's Witnesses say, the Holy Spirit certainly considers Himself a person and not a personification!

 The Holy Spirit's works confirm His personality. Besides having the attributes of personality, the Holy Spirit is seen doing many things in Scripture that only a person can do. For example, the Holy Spirit *teaches* believers (John 14:26), He *testifies* (John 15:26), He *guides* believers (Romans 8:14), He *commissions* people to service (Acts 13:4), He *issues commands* to believers (Acts 8:29), He *restrains sin* (Genesis 6:3), He *intercedes* (prays) for believers (Romans 8:26), and He *speaks* to people (John 15:26; 2 Peter 1:21).

Personal Intercession

Just as Christ (as a person) intercedes for believers (Hebrews 7:25), so the Holy Spirit (as a person) intercedes for believers (Romans 8:26). Both instances use the same Greek word for "intercede." A force cannot intercede or pray on behalf of another.

Challenge the Jehovah's Witness to reconcile the Watchtower Society view that the Holy Spirit is a "force" with the scriptural teaching that the Holy Spirit does things only a person can do, such as praying for believers, speaking to people, issuing commands, bearing witness, and teaching people.

The Holy Spirit is treated as a person. Scripture portrays the Holy Spirit being treated in a way that wouldn't make sense if He were not a person. Believers are encouraged, for example, not to *grieve* the Holy Spirit. If the Holy Spirit were a force (like electricity) or a thing (like my computer), why the concern about grieving it?

In Acts 5:3 we see that Ananias and Sapphira were guilty of *lying* to the Holy Spirit. It would not make any sense to view the Holy Spirit as a force, for we cannot lie to a force or a thing. (Imagine the strange looks you would get if you confessed at church that you lied to the electricity in your home that morning and sought forgiveness?) Only a *person* can be lied to.

Scripture portrays believers as *obeying* the Holy Spirit's commands and instructions. We noted earlier how Paul and Barnabas obeyed the Holy Spirit (Acts 13:2). Peter also obeyed the Holy Spirit in going to the house of Cornelius to share the gospel (Acts 10). A force or thing is not something that can be obeyed. Only a person can be obeyed. (One would never expect electricity to issue a command.)

The "lack of a name" argument is fallacious. The reality is that spiritual beings are not always named in Scripture. For example, evil spirits are rarely named in Scripture, but are identified by their particular character ("unclean," "wicked," and so forth—see Matthew 12:45). In the same way, by contrast, the Holy Spirit is identified by His primary character, which is holiness. To say the Holy Spirit is not a person because a name is not ascribed to Him is simply faulty reasoning.

The Holy Spirit is in fact related to the name of the other persons of the Trinity in Matthew 28:19: "Therefore go and make disciples of all nations, baptizing them in the name of the Father and of the Son and of the Holy Spirit." Just as the Father and the Son are persons, so the Holy Spirit is a person. All three are related by the same name.

Jehovah's Witnesses sometimes argue that the word "name" does not always mean *personal* name. For instance, when we say "in the name of the law," this is not referring to a person but what the law stands for. Witnesses claim that "name" is a common way of pointing to "power and authority."[8] They refer to this sense of the word in Matthew 28:19 and teach that this verse cannot be used to support belief in the personhood of the Holy Spirit.

In response, the New Testament Greek word for "name" is almost always used of real persons. Indeed, it is used 228 times in the New Testament, and except for four place names (Mark 14:32; Luke 1:26; 24:13; Acts 28:7), *always* refers to persons.[9] Especially since the word "name" in Matthew 28:19 is used in conjunction with the Father, Son, *and* Holy Spirit, it seems obvious that the personal element is present since the Father and the Son are undeniably persons.

The Watchtower Society's argument that the Holy Spirit cannot be a person since it "fills" many people is fallacious. It is highly revealing that Ephesians 3:19 speaks of God filling all the Ephesian believers. Likewise, Ephesians 4:10 speaks of Christ filling all things, and Ephesians 1:23 speaks of Christ as the one who "fills all in all." The fact that

God and Christ can fill all things does not mean they are not persons. In the same way, the fact that the Holy Spirit can "fill" numerous people does not prove He is not a person.

The Holy Spirit Is Both God and a Person

✓ Scripture identifies the Holy Spirit as God, ascribes the attributes of deity to Him, and portrays Him doing things only God can do.

✓ The Holy Spirit has all the attributes of personality (mind, emotions, and will).

✓ The Holy Spirit speaks of Himself as a person.

✓ The Holy Spirit does things only a person can do.

✓ The Holy Spirit is treated by others as only a person can be treated.

✓ The Holy Spirit interacts with others on a personal basis.

For further information on refuting the Watchtower view of the Holy Spirit, consult *Reasoning from the Scriptures with the Jehovah's Witnesses*, pp. 195-216.

6

The Biblical God
Is a Trinity

Jehovah's Witnesses believe that if people were to read the Bible from cover to cover without any preconceived ideas, they would never arrive at a belief in the Trinity. Witnesses argue that because God is not a God of disorder (1 Corinthians 14:33), Scripture would not speak of God in a way impossible to understand by human reason. According to them, the Trinity is incomprehensible so it cannot be correct. Moreover, they also point out that the word "Trinity" is not in the Bible.

The Watchtower Society views Satan as the true originator of the doctrine of the Trinity.[1] The doctrine is also said to be rooted in paganism. The Society argues that many centuries before the time of Christ, there were trinities of gods in ancient Babylonia, Egypt, and Assyria, so God would not be the author of such a belief.

Watchtower View of the Trinity

- The word "Trinity" is not found in the Bible.
- Because God is not a God of disorder, Scripture would not speak of God in a way impossible to understand by human reason.
- The doctrine of the Trinity is rooted in paganism and the work of the devil.

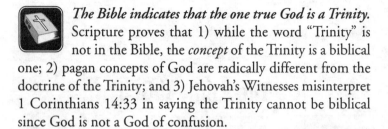

The Bible indicates that the one true God is a Trinity. Scripture proves that 1) while the word "Trinity" is not in the Bible, the *concept* of the Trinity is a biblical one; 2) pagan concepts of God are radically different from the doctrine of the Trinity; and 3) Jehovah's Witnesses misinterpret 1 Corinthians 14:33 in saying the Trinity cannot be biblical since God is not a God of confusion.

While the word "Trinity" is not in the Bible, the concept of the Trinity is a biblical one. The Jehovah's Witness may need to be reminded (or informed) that while the word "Jehovah" may be considered by some to be an acceptable way to render references to YHWH in the Old Testament (as does the American Standard Version of 1901), strictly speaking, Jehovah does not appear in any Hebrew or Greek manuscripts of the Bible.[2] "Jehovah" is a *manmade word.* Indeed, the ancient Jews inserted the vowels from Adonai (a-o-a) within the consonants, YHWH, resulting in *Yahowah* or *Jehovah.* They came up with this term as a substitute for God's name so they would not inadvertently break the Third Commandment. If it is going to be argued that the doctrine of the Trinity is unbiblical because the word "Trinity" does not appear in the Bible, then by that same logic the doctrine of Jehovah must be considered false. The important question is, Does the Bible teach the *concept?*

Naming Biblical Concepts

Just because a word is not in the Bible does not mean the concept intrinsic in that word is unbiblical. While the word "theocracy" is not in the Bible, the concept is. Israel was a "theocracy" since the word means "God-ruled nation." Interestingly, the Watchtower Society claims to be a "theocratic organization."

Throughout its history, the Watchtower Society has misrepresented the Trinity concept in order to make its denial of the doctrine plausible to reasonable people. For example, the Watchtower Society book *Studies in the Scriptures* (1899) said that "this doctrine of three Gods in one God...[is] one of the *dark mysteries* by which Satan, through the Papacy, has beclouded the Word and character of the plan of God."[3] (Trinitarians do not believe in "three Gods in one God"; they believe in *one* God and that three equal *persons* comprise the one Godhead.)

Elsewhere in this same volume is reference to "the unreasonable and unscriptural doctrine of the Trinity—three Gods in *one person*."[4] (Trinitarians do not believe the Trinity is "three Gods in one person"; they believe in three co-equal *persons* in the Godhead.)

One Watchtower book went so far as to refer to the Trinity as a freakish being:

> When the clergy are asked by their followers as to how such a combination of three in one can possibly exist, they are obliged to answer, "That is a mystery." Some will try to illustrate it by using triangles, trefoils, or images with three heads on one neck. Nevertheless, sincere persons who want to know the true God and serve him find it a bit difficult to love and worship a complicated, *freakish-looking, three-headed God.*[5]

 Be ready to provide the correct biblical definition of the Trinity and support it from Scripture. The doctrine of the Trinity is based on three lines of evidence: 1) there is only one true God; 2) there are three persons who are God; and 3) there is a three-in-oneness within the Godhead.

Evidence for One God

That there is only one true God is the consistent testimony of Scripture from Genesis to Revelation. It is a thread that runs through every page of the Bible. God positively affirmed through Isaiah the prophet: "This is what the LORD says—Israel's King and Redeemer, the LORD Almighty: I am the first and I am the last; apart from me there is no God" (Isaiah 44:6). God also said, "I am God, and there is no other; I am God, and there is none like me" (46:9).

The oneness of God is also often emphasized in the New Testament. In 1 Corinthians 8:4, for example, the apostle Paul asserted that "an idol is nothing at all in the world and that there is no God but one." James 2:19 says, "You believe that there is one God. Good! Even the demons believe that—and shudder." These and a multitude of other verses prove there is one—and only one—God.

Evidence for Three Persons Called God

On the one hand, Scripture says there is only one God. Yet in the unfolding of God's revelation to humankind, it also becomes clear that there are *three distinct persons* who are called God in Scripture.

- *The Father is God:* Peter refers to the saints "who have been chosen according to the foreknowledge of God the Father" (1 Peter 1:2).

- *Jesus is God:* When Jesus made a post-resurrection appearance to doubting Thomas, Thomas said: "My Lord and my God" (John 20:28). The heavenly Father said of His Son Jesus, "Your throne, O God, will last for ever and ever, and righteousness will be the scepter of your kingdom" (Hebrews 1:8).

- *The Holy Spirit is God:* In Acts 5:3,4, Peter said to Ananias, "How is it that Satan has so filled your heart that you have lied to the Holy Spirit?" Lying to the Holy Spirit is equated with lying to God.

Each of the three persons, on different occasions, is seen to possess the attributes of deity:

- *Omnipresence:* the Father (Jeremiah 23:23,24), the Son (Matthew 28:18), and the Holy Spirit (Psalm 139:7).
- *Omniscience:* the Father (Romans 11:33), the Son (Matthew 9:4), and the Holy Spirit (1 Corinthians 2:10).
- *Omnipotence:* the Father (1 Peter 1:5), the Son (Matthew 28:18), and the Holy Spirit (Romans 15:19).
- *Holiness:* the Father (Revelation 15:4), the Son (Acts 3:14), and the Holy Spirit (Romans 1:4).
- *Eternality:* the Father (Psalm 90:2), the Son (Micah 5:2; John 1:2; Revelation 1:8,17), and the Holy Spirit (Hebrews 9:14).
- *Truth:* the Father (John 7:28), the Son (Revelation 3:7), and the Holy Spirit (1 John 5:6).

After sharing the previous information, ask the Jehovah's Witness if he will concede that the Father, Son, and Holy Spirit each exercise the attributes of deity on different occasions. If he says no, look up some of the verses and *read them aloud.* Then ask, "Can anyone other than God have the *attributes* of God?" (Use this question to point to the deity of Jesus and the Holy Spirit, thus providing strong evidence for the doctrine of the Trinity.)

Three-in-Oneness in the Godhead. In the New American Standard Bible, Matthew 28:19 reads: "Go therefore and make disciples of all the nations, baptizing them in the name of *the* Father and *the* Son and *the* Holy Spirit" (emphasis added). It is highly revealing that the word "name" is singular in the Greek, indicating there is one God, but three distinct persons within the Godhead—*the* Father, *the* Son, and *the* Holy Spirit.[6] Theologian Robert Reymond draws our attention to the importance of this verse for the doctrine of the Trinity:

> Jesus does not say, (1) "into the names [plural] of the Father and of the Son and of the Holy Spirit," or what is its virtual equivalent, (2) "into the name of the Father, and into the name of the Son, and into the name of the Holy Spirit," as if we had to deal with three separate Beings. Nor does He say, (3) "into the name of the Father, Son, and Holy Spirit" (omitting the three recurring articles), as if "the Father, Son, and Holy Ghost" might be taken as merely three designations of a single person. What He does say is this: (4) "into the name [singular] of *the* Father, and of *the* Son, and of *the* Holy Spirit," first asserting the unity of the three by combining them all within the bounds of the single name, and then throwing into emphasis the distinctness of each by introducing them in turn with the repeated article.[7]

 Read Matthew 28:19 aloud from a reliable translation, and then focus attention on the fact that because the word "name" is singular in the Greek—and definite articles are placed in front of *the* Father, *the* Son, and *the* Holy Spirit—plurality within unity is thereby indicated. *God is a Trinity!*

Pagan concepts of God are radically different from the doctrine of the Trinity. The Babylonians and Assyrians believed in *triads* of gods who headed up a pantheon of many other gods. But these triads constituted three separate gods, which is utterly different from the doctrine of the Trinity, which maintains that there is only *one* God with *three* persons within the Godhead. Pagan practices, including polytheism, predate Christianity by some 2000 years and were far removed from the part of the world where Christianity emerged. From a historical and geographical perspective, the suggestion that Christianity borrowed the Trinitarian concept from pagans is quite unfeasible.

 It is interesting to note that many pagan religions taught the concepts of a great flood and a messiah-like figure ("Tammuz") who was resurrected. If the Watchtower Society uses a consistent method of reasoning, it must follow that the Christian doctrines of the flood, the Messiah (Jesus), and His resurrection are also pagan.[8]

Simply because pagans spoke of a concept remotely resembling something found in Scripture does not mean that the doctrine was stolen from pagans. If you can effectively make this point, the Jehovah's Witness will be forced to either admit the Society is wrong or conclude that the flood, the Messiah, and the resurrection of Christ are also derived from paganism.

 Jehovah's Witnesses misinterpret 1 Corinthians 14:33 in saying the Trinity cannot be biblical because God is not a God of confusion. Theologians often note that simply because we don't fully comprehend a doctrine does not mean the doctrine is false. For human beings to be able to understand everything about God, we would need to have the very mind of God. Scripture affirms:

- "Oh, the depth of the riches both of the wisdom and knowledge of God! How unsearchable are His judgments and unfathomable His ways!" (Romans 11:33 NASB).

- " 'For My thoughts are not your thoughts, nor are your ways My ways,' declares the LORD. 'For as the heavens are higher than the earth, so are My ways higher than your ways and My thoughts than your thoughts'" (Isaiah 55:8,9 NASB).

- "For now we see in a mirror dimly, but then face to face; now I know in part, but then I will know fully just as I also have been fully known" (1 Corinthians 13:12 NASB).

 Scripture is clear that human reasoning has limitations. Finite minds cannot possibly understand everything there is to know about an infinite being. Just as a young child cannot understand everything his father says and does, so we as God's children cannot understand everything about God.

What, then, did the apostle Paul mean when he said, "God is not a God of confusion but of peace"? Consulting the context of 1 Corinthians makes everything clear. The Corinthian church was plagued by internal divisions and disorder, especially in regard to the exercise of spiritual gifts. Since God is a God of peace, Paul says the church must model itself after God by seeking harmony in its services. By so doing, the church honors God. First Corinthians 14:33 doesn't even remotely deal with the Trinity.

The Biblical God Is a Trinity

✓ While the word "Trinity" is not in the Bible, the *concept* is biblical.

✓ Scripture indicates 1) there is one God; 2) three persons are called God (Father, Son, and Holy Spirit); and 3) there is three-in-oneness in the Godhead.

✓ The pagan triad view of God is polytheistic and is completely dissimilar to the doctrine of the Trinity.

✓ 1 Corinthians 14:33, in its reference to God not being a "God of confusion," relates not to the Trinity but to the abuse of spiritual gifts in the early church.

For further information on the Watchtower view of the Trinity, consult *Reasoning from the Scriptures with the Jehovah's Witnesses*, pp. 217-51.

Salvation Is by Grace Through Faith,
Not by Works

Though Jehovah's Witnesses often give lip service to the idea of salvation by grace through faith in Christ, in reality they believe in a works-oriented salvation. Salvation is impossible apart from total obedience to the Watchtower and vigorous participation in its various programs. Philippians 2:12 in the New World Translation reads, "Consequently, my beloved ones, in the way that you have always obeyed, not during my presence only, but now much more readily during my absence, keep *working* out your own salvation with fear and trembling." The Witnesses emphasize the necessity of good works. In the *Watchtower* magazine, one article included the statement that "to get one's name written in that Book of Life will depend upon one's works."[1] Witnesses are to continually be "working hard for the reward of eternal life."[2]

Part of a Jehovah's Witness "working out" his or her salvation involves faithfulness in distributing Watchtower literature door to door. Full-time "pioneer ministers" (committed Jehovah's Witnesses) can be required to spend up to 100 hours each month preaching from house to house and conducting home Bible studies.

Salvation Not Guaranteed

Jehovah's Witnesses cannot know for sure if they have attained salvation during this life. Only an unbending stance against sin and total obedience to the Watchtower give Witnesses any hope of salvation. Even then, they are told that if they should fail during the future millennium, they will be annihilated. However, if they faithfully serve God throughout this 1000-year period, eternal life may finally be granted.

Such a view minimizes the significance of Christ's sacrificial death. Indeed, the Watchtower Society often cites 1 Timothy 2:5,6—"For there is one God and one mediator between God and men, the man Christ Jesus, who gave himself as a ransom for all men..."—to argue that the human life Jesus laid down in sacrifice was *exactly equal* to the "human life" Adam fell with. "Since one man's sin (that of Adam) had been responsible for causing the entire human family to be sinners, the shed blood of another perfect human (in effect, a second Adam), being of corresponding value, could balance the scales of justice."[3] If Jesus had been God, we are told, the ransom payment would have been way too much.

Witnesses do speak of the need for grace and faith in Christ to be saved, and they speak of salvation as a "free gift." But obviously grace and faith are not enough in their religion. Nor is salvation really a free gift. Former Jehovah's Witness Duane Magnani explains it this way:

> What the Watchtower means by "free gift" is that Christ's death only wiped away the sin inherited from Adam. They teach that without this work of atonement, men could not work their way toward salvation. But the "gift" of Christ's ransom sacrifice is freely made available to all who desire it. In other words, without Christ's sacrifice, the individual wouldn't have a chance to get saved. But in view of His work, the free gift

which removed the sin inherited from Adam, the individual now has a chance.[4]

Watchtower Society View of Salvation

- Salvation is based on works and involves total obedience to the Watchtower Society.

- Distributing Watchtower literature door-to-door is pivotal in the salvation process.

- A person cannot be sure of salvation in this life.

- Jesus' work on the cross is downplayed. The human life Jesus laid down in sacrifice is said to be *exactly equal* to the human life Adam fell with.

- While salvation is said to be a free gift, in reality the "gift" is that the sin inherited from Adam has been wiped away. People now have the opportunity to work out their own salvation.

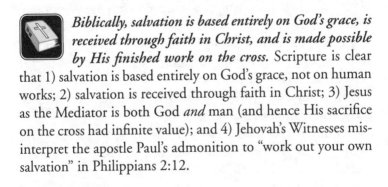

Biblically, salvation is based entirely on God's grace, is received through faith in Christ, and is made possible by His finished work on the cross. Scripture is clear that 1) salvation is based entirely on God's grace, not on human works; 2) salvation is received through faith in Christ; 3) Jesus as the Mediator is both God *and* man (and hence His sacrifice on the cross had infinite value); and 4) Jehovah's Witnesses misinterpret the apostle Paul's admonition to "work out your own salvation" in Philippians 2:12.

Salvation is based entirely on God's grace. "Grace" literally means "unmerited favor." The very definition of the word goes against the Watchtower Society's theology, for it refers to the *undeserved, unearned* favor of God. Romans 5:1-11 tells us that God gives His incredible grace to those who actually deserve the opposite—condemnation. "Unmerited" means this favor *cannot be worked for*. Indeed, if grace is not free, it is not truly grace. "If it is by grace, it is no longer on the basis of works, otherwise grace is no longer grace" (Romans 11:6 NASB).

Scripture is emphatic that eternal life cannot be earned. Verse after verse indicates that eternal life is a free gift that comes as a result of believing in the Savior, Jesus Christ. "The *free gift of God* is eternal life in Christ Jesus our Lord" (Romans 6:23 NASB, emphasis added). The resurrected Christ said, "I will give to the one who thirsts from the spring of the water of life *without cost*" (Revelation 21:6 NASB, emphasis added).

True grace is sometimes a hard concept for people to grasp, especially since our society is performance oriented. Good grades in school depend on how well we perform. Climbing up the corporate ladder at work depends on how well we perform. Nothing of any real worth is a "free ticket" in our society. But God's gift of salvation truly is a grace gift. *It is free!* We cannot attain it by a good performance. Ephesians 2:8,9 (NASB) affirms, "By grace you have been saved through faith; and that not of yourselves, it is the gift of God; not as a result of works, so that no one may boast." Titus 3:5 (NASB) tells us that God "saved us, not on the basis of deeds which we have done in righteousness, but according to His mercy."

By contrast, Romans 3:20 (NASB) asserts that "by the works of the Law no flesh will be justified [declared righteous] in His sight." In Galatians 2:16 (NASB) the apostle Paul tells us that "a man is not justified by the works of the Law but through faith in Christ Jesus." How desperately the Jehovah's Witness needs to hear this liberating news!

Gifts cannot be worked for; *only wages* can be worked for. As Romans 4:4,5 tells us, "When a man works, his wages are not credited to him as a gift, but as an obligation. However, to the man who does not work but trusts God who justifies the wicked, his faith is credited as righteousness." *Salvation is a free gift; it cannot be earned.*

 The person who seeks salvation through self-effort is like the man who, in attempting to sail across the Atlantic Ocean, found his sailboat becalmed for days with no wind. Finally, frustrated by his lack of progress, he tried to make his stalled sailboat move by pushing against the mast. Through strenuous effort, he succeeded in making the boat rock back and forth, and thereby created a few small waves on the otherwise smooth sea. Seeing the waves and feeling the rocking of the boat, he assumed he was making progress and so continued his efforts. However, though he exerted himself a great deal, he actually got nowhere

So it is with trying to work for our salvation. Our efforts to save ourselves are futile and exhausting. No matter how hard we try, it is no use. The source of salvation lies in God's grace alone, not in exertions of will-power, stabs at discipline, or any other self-effort. *Salvation is a free gift!* Clearly communicate this to your Jehovah's Witness friend.

 Salvation is received through faith in Christ. This is the consistent and unswerving testimony of the New Testament. Nearly 200 times in the New Testament, salvation is said to be by faith alone—with no works in sight. For example:

- John 3:15 tells us that "everyone who believes in [Jesus] may have eternal life."

- In John 11:25 Jesus says: "I am the resurrection and the life. He who believes in me will live, even though he dies."

- John 12:46 says: "I have come into the world as a light, so that no one who believes in me should stay in darkness."

- John 20:31 says: "But these are written that you may believe that Jesus is the Christ, the Son of God, and that by believing you may have life in his name."

Clearly, salvation is by faith in Christ! If this were not so, then Jesus' message in the Gospel of John—manifest in the previous quotations—would be deceptive. If salvation is obtained by both faith and good works, why would Jesus say so many times that there is only one condition for salvation—faith? He wouldn't!

Placing faith in Jesus Christ involves taking Him at His word. Faith involves believing that Christ is who He says He is. It also involves believing that He can do what He claims He can do—forgive us and come into our lives. Faith is an act of commitment in which we open the door of our hearts to Him.

Acts 16:30,31 in the New World Translation reads: "And he [the jailer] brought them [Paul and Silas] outside and said: 'Sirs, what must I do to get saved?' They said: 'Believe on the Lord Jesus and you will get saved, you and your household.'"

This verse illustrates two critically important facts: 1) Faith in Christ brings salvation, not good works; 2) Jesus is God. It may not be readily apparent that Jesus is God in this verse, but the context makes it clear. According to verse 31 the jailer was told that *believing in Jesus brings salvation.* Then verse 34 (NWT) tells us that the jailer "rejoiced greatly with all his household now that he had believed *God [Theos]*" (emphasis added). Contextually, believing in Jesus and believing in God are equated here. Stress this important truth to your friend.

 Jesus as the Mediator is both God and man. I noted earlier that Jehovah's Witnesses often cite 1 Timothy 2:5,6 in support of their view that Jesus paid a "corresponding ransom" for humankind. They argue that the human life Jesus laid down in sacrifice was *equal* to the human life Adam fell with.

The New American Standard Bible translates 1 Timothy 2:6 as indicating that Jesus "gave Himself as a ransom for all." The Greek word for ransom used here is *antilutron*. The question is, Does this word point to a "corresponding ransom" in the sense of "no more and no less" as the Watchtower Society argues? By no means! This is a case of *over*-translation; Witnesses are reading more into this word than is really there.[5] The word simply means "to give something in exchange for another thing as the price of redemption."

Substitution

Thayer's Greek Lexicon says that *antilutron,* the Greek word for "ransom," means "what is given in exchange for another as the price of his redemption, ransom."[6] The "ransom" in 1 Timothy 2:6 is called *antilutron* "in order to stress the fact of Christ's coming and suffering in the place of all and for their advantage."[7]

Jesus affirmed that it was for the very purpose of substitutionally dying that He came into the world (see John 12:27). At the last supper, Jesus gave His disciples the cup and said, "Drink from it, all of you. This is my blood of the covenant which is poured out for many for the forgiveness of sins" (Matthew 26:26-28). Jesus took His sacrificial mission with utmost seriousness. He knew that without Him, humanity would certainly perish (Matthew 16:25; John 3:16) and spend eternity apart from God in a place of great suffering (Matthew 10:28; 11:23; 23:33; 25:41; Luke 16:22-28).

Describing His mission, Jesus said: "The Son of Man did not come to be served, but to serve, and to give his life as a ransom for many" (Matthew 20:28); "the Son of Man came to seek and to save what was lost" (Luke 19:10); "for God did not send his Son into the world to condemn the world, but to save the world through him" (John 3:17). To properly appreciate these verses, we must keep in mind the Old Testament concept of substitution. The sacrificial victim had to be "without defect" (Leviticus 4:3,23,32). A hand would be laid on the unblemished sacrificial animal as a way of symbolizing a transfer of guilt (Leviticus 4:4,24,33). Note that the sacrificial animal did not become sinful by nature; rather, sin was *imputed* to the animal and the animal acted as a sacrificial substitute. In like manner, Christ the Lamb of God was *utterly unblemished* (1 Peter 1:19), but our sin was *imputed* to Him. He was our sacrificial substitute on the cross of Calvary.

The reason Christ's substitutionary work was so effective on our behalf is because of *who He is*. Humankind's redemption was completely dependent upon the human–divine union in Christ. If Christ the Redeemer had been *only* God, He could not have died, since God by His very nature cannot die. It was only as a human that Christ could represent us and die as a human. As God, however, Christ's death had infinite value more than sufficient to provide redemption for the sins of all humankind. Clearly, then, Christ had to be both God and man to secure our salvation.

Jehovah's Witnesses often argue that Jesus cannot be God since a mediator is by definition someone separate from those who need mediation (in this case, God and humankind).[8] The folly of this position is at once evident in the fact that if Jesus as mediator cannot be God, then, by the same logic, He cannot be human either. You might, therefore, ask the Jehovah's Witness: "If Christ *as a man* can be a mediator between God and man, then can't Christ *as God* also be a mediator between God and man?"

 Help your Jehovah's Witness acquaintance understand the Old Testament concept of the kinsman-redeemer. In Old Testament times, the phrase "kinsman-redeemer" was always used of one who was related by blood to someone he was seeking to redeem from bondage. If someone was sold into slavery, for example, it was the duty of a blood relative—the "next of kin"—to act as that person's "kinsman-redeemer" and buy him out of slavery (Leviticus 25:47,48).

Jesus is the Kinsman-Redeemer for sin-enslaved humanity. For Jesus to become a kinsman-redeemer, however, He had to become *related by blood* to the human race. This indicates the necessity of the Incarnation. Jesus became a man in order to redeem humanity (Hebrews 2:14-16). And because Jesus was also fully God, His sacrificial death had infinite value (9:11-28). His ransom was effective precisely because of who the Ransomer was.

 Jehovah's Witnesses misinterpret the apostle Paul's admonition to "work out your own salvation." Philippians 2:12 says, "Therefore, my dear friends, as you have always obeyed—not only in my presence, but now much more in my absence—continue to work out your salvation with fear and trembling." Contexually, this verse has nothing to do with assurance of final salvation for individual believers.

As a backdrop, we should keep in mind the particular situation of the church in Philippi. This church was plagued by: 1) rivalries and individuals with personal ambition (Philippians 2:3,4; 4:2); 2) the teaching of Judaizers who said circumcision was necessary for salvation (3:1-3); 3) perfectionism—the view that a person could attain sinless perfection in this life (3:12-14); and 4) the influence of "antinomian libertines," people who took excessive liberty in how they lived their lives, ignoring or going against God's law (3:18,19).[9] Because of such problems, this church *as a unit* was in need of "salvation"—salvation in the *temporal, experiential* sense, not in the *eternal* sense.

It is critical to recognize that salvation in this context is in reference to the *community* of believers in Philippi and not to *individual* believers. Salvation is spoken of in a *corporate* sense in this verse. The Philippians were called by the apostle Paul to "keep on working out" (continuously) the "deliverance of the church into a state of Christian maturity."[10]

The Greek word for "work out" *(katergazomai)* is a compound verb that indicates *achievement* or *bringing to a conclusion.* Paul was calling the Philippians to solve all the church's problems, thus bringing corporate salvation or deliverance to a state of final achievement. Paul would not permit things to continue as they were. The problems must be solved. The Philippians were to "work it out to the finish."[11]

The Philippians were to accomplish their appointed task with an attitude of "fear and trembling." This does not mean Paul wanted the Philippians to have terror in their hearts as a motivation. Rather, the words "fear and trembling" are an idiomatic expression pointing to great reverence for God and a humble frame of mind. Such humility and reverence for God would help them overcome the problems they were experiencing in the church (compare with 1 Corinthians 2:3; 2 Corinthians 7:15; Ephesians 6:5). (Remember—many in Philippi were prideful and had little reverence for God.)

Aside from the above, the Watchtower Society's interpretation of Philippians 2:12 clearly goes against what the rest of the Bible says on the issue of salvation (see Psalm 37:23,24; 138:8; John 5:24; 6:37-40; 10:27-30; 17:8-11; Romans 5:1-5; 1 Corinthians 1:8,9; 2 Corinthians 1:21,22; Ephesians 1:4,5; Philippians 1:6; 1 Thessalonians 5:23,24; 2 Timothy 1:12; 4:18; 1 Peter 1:3-5; 5:10; 1 John 2:1,2; 5:10-18; Jude 1).

 Help your Jehovah's Witness acquaintance see that in other writings of the apostle Paul, salvation by grace through faith alone is taught (see, for example, Ephesians 2:8,9). Also point out that he clearly teaches "eternal security" in salvation. For example, in Romans 8:29,30 (NKJV) Paul said, "For whom He foreknew, He also predestined to be conformed to the image of His Son...[and] whom He predestined, these He also called; whom He called, these He also justified; and whom He justified, these He also glorified." Here we find an unbroken progression from predestination to glorification. And the tense of the word "glorified" (in the Greek) indicates that our future glorification is *so certain* for those who trust in Christ that it can be said to be already accomplished.

Another Pauline evidence for eternal security is found in Ephesians 4:30, where we are told that believers are "sealed" by the Holy Spirit for the day of redemption. A seal indicates *possession* and *security*. "The presence of the Holy Spirit, the seal, is the believer's guarantee of the security of his salvation."[12]

The believer in Christ is assured that he or she will, in fact, be with God in heaven for all eternity.

Salvation Is by Grace Through Faith Alone

✓ Salvation is based entirely upon God's grace ("unmerited favor"), not human works.

✓ Salvation is received through faith in Christ.

✓ Jesus as the Mediator is both God *and* man; therefore, His sacrifice on the cross had infinite value.

✓ Jehovah's Witnesses misinterpret Paul's admonition to "work out your own salvation" in Philippians 2:12.

For further information on refuting the Watchtower view of salvation, consult *Reasoning from the Scriptures with the Jehovah's Witnesses*, pp. 283-304.

8

There Is One People of God—
Not Two Peoples with Different Destinies

 In Watchtower theology there are two classes of saved people with two very different destinies and sets of privileges: the privileged "Anointed Class" and the lesser "other sheep."

The Anointed Class

The Watchtower Society teaches that only 144,000 Jehovah's Witnesses go to heaven—and these people make up the Anointed Class (the 144,000 are mentioned in Revelation 7:4 and 14:1–3).[1] Only those who become "born again"—thereby becoming "sons" of God—can share in this heavenly kingdom (drawing on John 1:12,13; Romans 8:16,17; 1 Peter, chapters 3 and 4). These individuals look forward not to physical existence but to spiritual existence in heaven.

Only a relative few find entrance into this spiritual kingdom—and they are a "little flock" when compared with Earth's population. This "little flock" of true believers allegedly began with the 12 apostles and other Christians of the first century and was completely filled by the year 1935. (Watchtower leader Judge Rutherford allegedly received a "revelation" to this effect.) Less than 4,000 of these "anointed" believers are still alive today.

The Watchtower Society teaches that only the Anointed Class...

- become born again (John 3:3-8)
- are heirs with Christ (Romans 8:17)
- are baptized in the Holy Spirit (1 Corinthians 12:13)
- take the Lord's Supper (1 Corinthians 11:20-29)
- live in heaven (1 Corinthians 15:50)
- will rule with Christ (Revelation 20:6)

The primary activity of the Anointed Class in heaven will be to rule with Christ as "kings" (derived from Revelation 20:6). Obviously, if the Anointed Class is made up of kings, there must be others over whom the Anointed Class will rule.[2] These are the "other sheep" who have an earthly destiny.

The Other Sheep

Jehovah's Witnesses who are not members of the Anointed Class look forward not to a heavenly destiny but to living eternally on an earthly paradise. They believe verses such as Psalm 37:9,11,29 indicate that God has forever given the earth to humankind for this purpose: "For evil men will be cut off, but those who hope in the LORD will inherit the land"; "but the meek will inherit the land and enjoy great peace"; "the righteous will inherit the land and dwell in it forever." Since the required number of 144,000 members for the Anointed Class became a reality in 1935, *all* Jehovah's Witnesses since that year have looked forward to an earthly destiny.

These individuals are what Revelation 7:9 calls the "great multitude" and John 10:16 calls the "other sheep." These are followers of Jesus Christ who are not in the "New Covenant sheepfold" with a hope of heavenly life. They hope to survive the approaching Great Tribulation and Armageddon, and then enjoy perfect human life on earth under the rule of Christ. Those of the "other sheep" who have died will experience a "resurrection of life" and will fully enjoy earthly blessings.

Two Peoples of God

- The Anointed Class is made up of 144,000 privileged Jehovah's Witnesses who enjoy a spiritual existence in heaven and participate in ruling with Christ.

- The "other sheep" refers to all other Jehovah's Witnesses who live forever on a paradise Earth in subjection to Christ and the Anointed Class.

Biblically, there are not two peoples of God with two different destinies; rather, there is one people of God who will live in heaven for eternity. The key points to cover are: 1) Jehovah's Witnesses misunderstand what the Bible says about the 144,000 (Revelation 7:4; 14:1-3) and the "little flock" (Luke 12:32); 2) the experience of becoming "born again" is for *all* believers in Christ, not for a select subcategory of believers; 3) Jehovah's Witnesses misunderstand the identity of the "other sheep" and the "great multitude" (John 10:16; Revelation 7:9); 4) Jehovah's Witnesses misunderstand Psalm 37:9,11,29, which speaks of God giving the earth to humankind; and 5) Scripture consistently speaks of *one* people of God who forever exist in the *same* location—with God in heaven.

Jehovah's Witnesses misunderstand what the Bible says about the 144,000 and the "little flock." Since their understanding of individual Scripture verses is flawed, Jehovah Witnesses reach an inaccurate conclusion regarding "two peoples of God."

The 144,000

The Book of Revelation speaks of the 144,000 in terms of the 12 tribes of Israel, with 12,000 in each tribe:

> Then I heard the number of those who were sealed: 144,000 from all the tribes of Israel. From the tribe of Judah 12,000 were sealed, from the tribe of Reuben 12,000, from the tribe of Gad, 12,000, from the tribe of Asher 12,000, from the tribe of Naphtali 12,000, from the tribe of Manasseh 12,000, from the tribe of Simeon 12,000, from the tribe of Levi 12,000, from the tribe of Issachar 12,000, from the tribe of Zebulun 12,000, from the tribe of Joseph 12,000, from the tribe of Benjamin 12,000 (Revelation 7:4-8).

The Watchtower Society (WS) says this is actually a metaphorical reference to the Anointed Class of believers who have a heavenly destiny. The WS says these people cannot be the tribes of natural Israel because there never was a tribe of Joseph in the Old Testament, even though one is mentioned in Revelation 7:4-8. As well, the tribes of Ephraim and Dan, which were tribes of Israel in the Old Testament, are not included in the list in Revelation 7. Further, the Levites, who are mentioned as being a tribe in Revelation 7, were set aside for service in connection with the temple in the Old Testament but were not reckoned as one of the 12 tribes.[3] Clearly, according to the WS, the 144,000 in Revelation 7 are not *literally* the 12 tribes of

Israel. This passage refers not to natural Israelites but to the Anointed Class of 144,000 consecrated Jehovah's Witnesses.

In response, there is a very good reason to interpret this verse as referring literally to 144,000 Jews, 12,000 from each tribe. Nowhere else in the Bible does a reference to "12 tribes of Israel" mean *anything but* the 12 tribes of Israel. The word "tribes" is never used of anything but a specific ethnic group in Scripture.

In support of the literal interpretation is the fact that Jesus spoke of the 12 apostles (whom we know were real people) sitting on "twelve thrones, judging the twelve tribes of Israel" in the last day (Matthew 19:28). Like Revelation 7, there is no reason not to take this literally.

 The Watchtower switches interpretive methodology right in the middle of Revelation 7:4. Notice that the first half of the verse is interpreted using a *literal* method of interpretation: "And I heard the number of those who were sealed, *one hundred and forty-four thousand...*" (emphasis added). It is thus concluded by Jehovah's Witnesses that the Anointed Class will have *precisely* 144,000 people. But then the second half of the verse *is not* interpreted literally: "...sealed from every tribe of the sons of Israel." The Watchtower Society argues that there are literally 144,000, then goes nonliteral to interpret the 144,000 as the Anointed Class of Jehovah's Witnesses. Confront the Jehovah's Witness on this inconsistency.

It is highly relevant to our discussion that women are excluded from this group of 144,000.[4] In referring to this group, Revelation 14:4 (NASB) says: "These are the ones who have *not been defiled with women,* for they have kept themselves chaste" (emphasis added). This means either that the 144,000 men are unmarried or they are celibate (see 2 Corinthians

11:2). Either way, the fact that they "have not been defiled with women," and the fact that masculine pronouns are used of this group, shows that they are men. To try to argue that women can be part of this group (as the Watchtower Society consistently does) is to ignore the clear teaching of Scripture. In context, these are 144,000 Jewish *men* who become believers during the future Tribulation period, and who evangelize all over the world.

What about the WS contention that the tribes mentioned in Revelation 7 cannot be literal tribes of Israel because the Old Testament tribes of Dan and Ephraim are omitted? The fact is that the Old Testament contains some 20 variant lists of tribes. No single list of the 12 tribes of Israel must be identical.[5]

Dan's tribe was no doubt omitted in Revelation because that tribe was guilty of idolatry on many occasions and, as a result, was largely obliterated (see Leviticus 24:11; Judges 18:1,30; 1 Kings 12:28,29). To engage in unrepentant idolatry is to be cut off from God's blessing. Ephraim's tribe, too, was involved in idolatry and paganized worship (see Judges 17; Hosea 4:17). Since Dan and Ephraim were omitted because of idolatry, the readjustment of the list to include Joseph and Manasseh to complete the 12 makes good sense.[6]

Why was the tribe of Levi included in the listing of tribes in Revelation 7, rather than maintaining its special status as a priestly tribe under the Mosaic Law? Probably because the priestly functions of the tribe of Levi *ceased* with the coming of Christ—the ultimate High Priest.[7] Indeed, the Levitical priesthood was *fulfilled* in the Person of Christ (Hebrews 7–10).[8] Because there was no further need for the services of the tribe of Levi as priests, there was no further reason for keeping this tribe distinct and separate, so they were properly included in the tribal listing in Revelation.

Conclusion: The Watchtower's objections to interpreting the tribes of Revelation 7 and 14 as literal tribes of Israel are without warrant. The view that the 144,000 refers to the Anointed Class is completely without biblical support.

The "Little Flock"

Luke 12:32 (NIV) reads: "Do not be afraid, little flock, for your Father has been pleased to give you the kingdom." The little flock, according to Jehovah's Witnesses, is made up of 144,000 people who have a heavenly destiny. A look at the context, however, reveals that Luke 12:22-34 (all 13 verses!) is a *single* unit, beginning with: "Then Jesus said to his disciples..." (verse 22). The *entire unit*—from verses 22 to 34—contains words spoken by Jesus *directly to His earthly disciples* in the first century. By no stretch of the imagination can this passage be made to relate to a select group of 144,000 members of an "Anointed Class" that would develop from the first century to 1935.

 Jesus' Disciples—His "Sheep"

Jesus elsewhere referred to His disciples as sheep in His flock:

- "Behold, I send you out as sheep in the midst of wolves..." (Matthew 10:16 NASB).

- Regarding the crucifixion: "You will all fall away because of Me this night, for it is written, 'I will strike down the shepherd, and the sheep of the flock shall be scattered'" (Matthew 26:31 NASB).

Contextually, in Luke 12:22-34 Jesus is instructing the disciples not to worry about food, clothing, and other things. Worry is senseless because it does not accomplish anything (verses 25,26). Worrying will not extend anyone's life a single day, and the root of worry is a lack of faith (verse 29). The disciples were to keep in mind that God the Father knows what they need (verse 30). Jesus said that if they would simply commit to making the kingdom their consuming passion, then God would take care of all their other needs: "But seek his kingdom, and these things will be added to you" (verse 31). The disciples (Christ's "sheep") were not to fear but were to trust in God, for "your Father has chosen gladly to give you the kingdom" (verse 32 NASB).

Conclusion: In context, there is no basis for relating these verses to 144,000 members of an "Anointed Class."

 The experience of becoming "born again" is for all believers in Christ. While Jehovah's Witnesses speak of being "born again" (John 3:3-5), they do not interpret this as evangelical Christians do. They say the new birth is for the Anointed Class only. The Watchtower Society teaches that this new birth is necessary so they can enjoy spirit life in heaven; but such a "new birth" is not necessary for the "other sheep," for they will live forever on a paradise Earth.[9]

 Contrary to the Watchtower view, 1 John 5:1 (NASB) affirms that "whoever believes that Jesus is the Christ is born of God." Being born again cannot be limited to 144,000 people. This is in perfect keeping with Jesus' discussion of being "born again" with Nicodemus (John 3:1-21). After saying that one must be born again (verses 3,7), Jesus said, "For God so loved the world, that He gave His only begotten Son, that *whoever believes in Him* shall not perish, but have eternal life" (verse 16 NASB, emphasis added). John 1:12,13 agrees: "But *as many as received Him*, to them He gave the right to become children of God, *even to those who believe in His name*, who were born not of blood nor of the will of the flesh nor of the will of man, but of God" (NASB, emphasis added). Help your Jehovah's Witness acquaintance understand the universal nature of these key verses.

"Born Again"

Being "born again" (literally, "born from above") refers to the act of God by which He gives eternal life to any person who believes in Christ (Titus 3:5,6). Being born again places believers in God's eternal family (1 Peter 1:23) and gives them a new capacity and desire to please the Father.

In John 3:6 (NASB), Jesus asserts to Nicodemus: "That which is born of the flesh is flesh, and that which is born of the Spirit is spirit." The *flesh* includes not only what is *natural* but what is *sinful* in humanity—that is, people as they are born into this fallen world, living their lives apart from God's grace. Flesh can only reproduce itself as flesh, and this cannot pass muster with God (Romans 8:8). The law of reproduction is "after its kind." So likewise the Spirit produces spirit—a life *born, nurtured,* and *matured* by the Spirit of God.[10] This experience of fallen mankind receiving eternal life from God is open to *all* who believe in Christ (see John 1:12,13).

In Nicodemus' case, we find a Pharisee who would have been trusting in his physical descent from Abraham for entrance into the Messiah's kingdom. The Jews believed that because they were physically related to Abraham, they were in a privileged position before God. Christ, however, denied such a possibility. Parents can give their children only the nature which they themselves possess (that is, a *sinful* nature). The only way a person can enter God's kingdom is to experience a spiritual rebirth, and this is precisely what Jesus is emphasizing to Nicodemus. *All* who trust in Jesus receive the "new birth."

Jehovah's Witnesses misunderstand the identity of the "other sheep" and the "great multitude." And since their understanding of John 10:16 and Reveation 7:9

is flawed, their conclusion that Scripture teaches "two peoples of God" is naturally flawed.

The "Other Sheep"

John 10:16 (NASB) reads: "I have *other sheep*, which are not of this fold; I must bring them also, and they will hear My voice; and they will become one flock with one shepherd" (emphasis added). The Jehovah's Witnesses teach that though there are only 144,000 spirit-anointed believers who go to heaven, God has "other sheep," *other* true believers, who will receive eternal life and live on an earthly paradise.

Contrary to the Watchtower view, the context in John 10 indicates that the "other sheep" are *Gentile* believers as opposed to *Jewish* believers. The unbelieving Jews in the Gospels are referred to as "the lost sheep of Israel" (Matthew 10:6; 15:24). The Jews who followed Christ were called *His* "sheep" (John 10). When Jesus said "I have other sheep," He was clearly referring to non-Jewish, Gentile believers. Jesus thus affirmed that the Gentile believers, along with the Jewish believers, "shall become one flock with one shepherd" (not one flock on earth and one flock in heaven) (see John 10:16).

The "Great Multitude"

Revelation 7:9 (NASB) states, "After these things I looked, and behold, a *great multitude which no one could count,* from every nation and all tribes and peoples and tongues, standing before the throne and before the Lamb, clothed in white robes, and palm branches were in their hands" (emphasis added). The Watchtower Society argues that this verse refers to the "other sheep" mentioned in John 10:16. This great multitude will allegedly live forever on a paradise Earth.

Contextually, the "great multitude" refers to those who become Christians during the future Tribulation period

(Revelation 7:14 makes this clear) and, hence, have a destiny of heaven. Contrary to the Watchtower Society's position, *nowhere in the text of Revelation* does it say this "great multitude" is exempt from heaven and will live forever on a paradise Earth. This is something the Witnesses read into the text.

Revelation 7:9 explicitly refers to this group "standing before the throne and before the Lamb." The "great multitude" is *physically present* before God's throne in heaven, just as the angels are before God's throne (verse 11). This alone shows the unfeasibility of interpreting the great multitude as living forever on a paradise Earth.

"Before" God's Throne

Revelation 7:9 says the great multitude is "before" God's throne. The Greek word in question literally carries the idea *"of place,* before someone or something."[11] In Revelation 7:9 it refers to being *in the physical presence of God's throne,* not being "spiritually before" God on earth, as Jehovah's Witnesses argue.

In keeping with this, Revelation 7:15 (NASB) says of this multitude: "For this reason, they are before the throne of God; and they serve Him day and night in His temple." Where is God's "temple" located? Revelation 11:19 (NASB) refers to "the temple of God which is in heaven." Revelation 14:17 likewise says: "And another angel came out of the temple which is in heaven...."

The great multitude is said to be "before the throne," "before the Lamb," and they serve God day and night "in His temple" which is "in heaven" (Revelation 7:9,15; 11:19; 14:17). Ask the Jehovah's Witness to defend the idea *(with scriptural support)* that this great multitude lives forever on a paradise earth.

Jehovah's Witnesses misunderstand the meaning of Psalm 37:9,11,29, which speaks of God giving the earth to humankind. The New World Translation renders Psalm 37:9,11,29 this way: "For evildoers themselves will be cut off, but those hoping in Jehovah are the ones that *will possess the earth*....But the meek ones themselves *will possess the earth*, and they will indeed find their exquisite delight in the abundance of peace....The righteous themselves *will possess the earth*, and they will reside forever upon it" (emphasis added). These verses allegedly prove that some of God's people will live forever on a paradise Earth.

A look at the context of Psalm 37, however, reveals that the psalm is not referring to a distant future when God will remove all the wicked people and allow good people to live on a paradise Earth. Rather, the psalmist was speaking of something that people *in his own lifetime* (and the following generations) would experience. The psalmist was indicating that evil people *in his time* would be cut off from the Promised Land; righteous people *in his time* would experience blessing in the Promised Land.[12]

It is critical to recognize that the Hebrew word for "earth" in this context has reference to *land*—more specifically, the land of Judea that God promised to the Jewish patriarchs.[13] In other words, it refers to the Promised Land given as an inheritance to the people of God. The verses indicate that the righteous will inherit the land while the wicked will be cut off from it.[14]

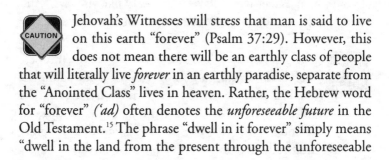 Jehovah's Witnesses will stress that man is said to live on this earth "forever" (Psalm 37:29). However, this does not mean there will be an earthly class of people that will literally live *forever* in an earthly paradise, separate from the "Anointed Class" lives in heaven. Rather, the Hebrew word for "forever" *('ad)* often denotes the *unforeseeable future* in the Old Testament.[15] The phrase "dwell in it forever" simply means "dwell in the land from the present through the unforeseeable

future." The phrase is a Hebrew way of saying that the *then living* Israelites would dwell in the Promised Land their entire lives *as would their children and their children's children* and so forth. From one generation to the next, the righteous would experience blessing in the Promised Land. This is in noted contrast to the wicked; for, as the previous verse points out, "The offspring of the wicked will be cut off" (verse 28).

 Scripture consistently speaks of one people of God who forever exist with God in heaven. Never once did Jesus restrict the kingdom of God to a specific number of people, as Jehovah's Witnesses do. He taught that *all* people should seek the kingdom, and said that *whoever* sought it would find it (see Matthew 9:35-38; Mark 1:14,15; Luke 12:22-34).

 Point out the following scriptural facts to your Jehovah's Witness acquaintance:

- It is the clear testimony of Scripture that a heavenly destiny awaits *all* who believe in Christ, not just a select group of 144,000 (Ephesians 2:19; Philippians 3:20; Colossians 3:1-4; Hebrews 3:1; 12:22; 2 Peter 1:10,11).

- *All who believe in Christ* are heirs of the eternal kingdom (Galatians 3:29; 4:28-31; Titus 3:7; James 2:5).

- The righteousness of God that leads to life in heaven is available "through faith in Jesus Christ *to all who believe.* There is no difference" (Romans 3:22, emphasis added).

- Jesus promised: "If *anyone* serves Me, he must follow Me; and where I am, there My servant will be also [that is, heaven]" (John 12:26, emphasis added).

• Jesus affirmed that *all* believers will be together in "one flock" under "one shepherd" (John 10:16).

There Are Not Two Peoples of God with Two Different Destinies

✓ The 144,000 in Revelation 7 and 14 refers not to an elite subcategory of Jehovah's Witnesses, but to Jews who become Christians in the end times and evangelize during the future Tribulation period.

✓ The experience of being "born again" is for all who believe in Christ, not for an "Anointed Class" of believers.

✓ Jehovah's Witnesses misinterpret references to the "other sheep," the "great multitude," and the "little flock." They are practicing *eisogesis* (reading meaning *into* the text).

✓ There are not two peoples of God, but rather one people of God with one destiny—*heaven.*

For further information on refuting the Watchtower view of two peoples of God, consult *Reasoning from the Scriptures with the Jehovah's Witnesses,* pp. 253-81.

Man
Is Conscious in the Afterlife, and Hell Is a Real Place of Eternal Suffering

Jehovah's Witnesses do not believe a person's soul or spirit is distinct from the physical body. In their thinking, the "soul" refers not to an "immaterial" part of a human that survives death, but to the very life a person has. According to the Watchtower Society, every person is a "soul" not because he or she possesses an unseen nature but because he or she is a living being (Genesis 9:5).

Witnesses typically cite Genesis 2:7 in support of their view. The New World Translation renders this verse: "And Jehovah God proceeded to form the man out of dust from the ground and to blow into his nostrils the breath of life, and *the man came to be a living soul*" (emphasis added). This verse is said to prove that man is a combination of physical material and "breath," which together form a living soul.

Jehovah's Witnesses also cite Luke 23:46, which informs us that Jesus, after saying to the Father "into your hands I entrust my spirit," expired. They argue that the man Jesus was a mortal and did not have an immortal soul that consciously survived death. He entrusted His "spirit" to the Father in the sense that

He knew that when He died, His future life prospects rested entirely with God.[1]

The doctrine of the soul closely relates to the question of what happens at death. Because of the inheritance of sin from Adam, Witnesses believe human beings die and return to the dust just as animals do. They do not possess a spirit that goes on living as an intelligent personality after death. Man's "spirit" is interpreted as the "life-force" within him, and at death that life-force wanes.

Jehovah's Witnesses often cite verses such as Psalm 146:3,4 to prove that at death, consciousness ceases. The New World Translation renders this passage: "Do not put your trust in nobles, nor in the son of earthling man, to whom no salvation belongs. His spirit goes out, he goes back to his ground; in that day *his thoughts do perish*" (emphasis added). They also typically cite Ecclesiastes 9:5, which in the New World Translation reads: "For the living are conscious that they will die; but as for the dead, *they are conscious of nothing at all*" (emphasis added).

Since at death man has no immaterial nature that survives, he is obviously not conscious of anything following death. "When a person is dead he is completely out of existence. He is not conscious of anything."[2] Even for the righteous, the dead remain unconscious and inactive in the grave until the time of the future resurrection. People also don't consciously suffer in hell. Satan, the father of lies, is said to be behind this concept. Hell is redefined as the common grave of all humankind.[3] The wicked are *annihilated*.

Watchtower View of the Afterlife

- Man does not have a separate "immaterial" nature known as the soul.

- The soul refers to the life-force within a person. At death, that life-force wanes.

- There is no conscious existence following the moment of death.

• Hell is not a place of eternal suffering; it is simply the common grave of humankind.

 From a biblical perspective, the Watchtower Society's view of the afterlife is permeated with error. Scripture reveals that 1) the verses Jehovah's Witnesses cite to prove the "soul" is merely a life-force are taken out of context; 2) man has a conscious immaterial nature that survives death; 3) the verses Jehovah's Witnesses cite to prove that consciousness vanishes at death are taken out of context; and 4) hell is a place of eternal, conscious suffering.

 The verses Jehovah's Witnesses cite to prove the "soul" is merely a life-force are taken out of context. Since their interpretation of these verses is flawed, the conclusion they draw on the nature of the soul in the afterlife is flawed as well.

As noted previously, Genesis 2:7 in the New World Translation reads: "And Jehovah God proceeded to form the man out of dust from the ground and to blow into his nostrils the breath of life, and *the man came to be a living soul*" (emphasis added). It is true that the Hebrew word for soul *(nephesh)* can be used in the Old Testament in reference to a living being.[4] Genesis 2:7 is an example of this. But because the word is used in this sense in 2:7 does not mean the word is *limited* to this or that mankind does not have an immaterial nature.

The same word can have different meanings in different contexts. In English, for example, the word "trunk" can refer to an elephant's nose, the back of a car, the bottom of a tree, or a suitcase, depending on the context. Biblically, the best policy is to examine how the word "soul" is variously used throughout Scripture. When that is done, it becomes clear that one of the meanings of the word has to do with one's immaterial nature that is distinct from the body.

Besides referring to "living beings" (as in the case in Genesis 2:7), *nephesh* (soul) is also in the Old Testament to refer to the seat of emotions and experiences. Man's *nephesh* can be sad (Deuteronomy 28:65), grieved (Job 30:25), distressed (Genesis 42:21), bitter (Job 3:20), troubled (Psalm 6:3), and cheered (Psalm 86:4).

In this sense, the word seems to refer to the "inner man" within a human being. This is in keeping with verses such as 2 Kings 4:27 (NASB), "The man of God said, 'Let her alone, for her soul is troubled *within* her....'" Likewise, Psalm 42:6 says, "O my God, my soul is in despair *within* me," and Psalm 43:5 says, "Why are you in despair, O my soul? And why are you disturbed *within* me?" (emphasis added in these verses).

In Genesis 35:18, *nephesh* can be interpreted to refer to man's immaterial nature: "It came about *as her soul was departing* (for she died), that she named him Ben-oni; but his father called him Benjamin."[5] This verse seems to recognize the soul as distinct from the physical body which dies, for at death the soul "departs" from the body.

 Man has a conscious immaterial nature (a "soul") that survives death. As stated previously, one of the most important principles of Bible interpretation is that Scripture interprets Scripture. The interpretation of a specific passage must not contradict the total teaching of Scripture on a point. Individual texts do not exist as isolated fragments, but as parts of a whole. The exposition of these texts must involve exhibiting them in right relation both to the whole and to each other. By comparing Scripture with Scripture, it becomes quite evident that while Genesis 2:7 says only that man became a "living being," other passages in Scripture clearly point to man's immaterial nature.

Revelation 6:9,10

In this passage we read: "When he opened the fifth seal, I saw under the altar *the souls of those who had been slain* because of the word of God and the testimony they had maintained. They called out in a loud voice, 'How long, Sovereign Lord, holy and true, until you judge the inhabitants of the earth and avenge our blood?'" (emphasis added). In this case it is impossible that the "soul" refers to "living being"—for then the text would read, "I saw underneath the altar the *living beings* of those who had been slain."[6] Notice that the souls exist and are conscious despite the fact that they had been physically slain.

Since these individuals had been *physically* slain, and since their "souls" are portrayed as *conscious* in God's presence, doesn't this indicate an immaterial nature that survives physical death? This is a good question to ask a Jehovah's Witness.

Luke 23:46

"'Father, into your hands I commit my spirit.' When he had said this, he breathed his last." These were Jesus' words on the cross. The Greek word translated "spirit" in this verse is *pneuma,* which has a wide range of meanings including "wind," "breath," "life-spirit," "soul," "the spirit as a part of the human personality," "the spirit of God," "the spirit of Christ," and "the Holy Spirit."[7] Many of these meanings are disqualified as possible contenders for Luke 23:46 by the context. It would not make sense for Jesus to commend His "wind" or His "breath" to the Father. Nor would it fit the context for Jesus to commit "the spirit of God" or "the Holy Spirit" to the Father. The only meanings of *pneuma* that contextually make sense are "soul" and "spirit as a part of the human personality." It seems clear from a plain reading of the verse that Jesus is committing His human immaterial soul, or spirit, to the Father.

Acts 7:59

"They went on stoning Stephen as he called on the Lord and said, 'Lord Jesus, receive my spirit!'" (NASB). This verse would make no sense if we interpret "spirit" as the life-force within Stephen that would cease to exist at the moment of death. Why would Stephen ask Jesus to receive that which was about to cease existing? Stephen is clearly asking Jesus to receive to Himself that part of him that would survive the death of his physical body.

1 Thessalonians 4:13-17

> Brothers, we do not want you to be ignorant about *those who fall asleep*, or to grieve like the rest of men, who have no hope. We believe that Jesus died and rose again and so we believe that God will *bring with Jesus those who have fallen asleep* in him. According to the Lord's own word, we tell you that we who are still alive, who are left till the coming of the Lord, will certainly not precede *those who have fallen asleep.* For the Lord himself will come down from heaven, with a loud command, with the voice of the archangel and with the trumpet call of God, and the *dead in Christ will rise first.* After that, we who are still alive and are left will be caught up together with them in the clouds to meet the Lord in the air. And so we will be with the Lord forever.

Though the term "sleep" is often used to denote death in Scripture, it is never used in reference to the soul of man. Indeed, "sleep" is always applied in Scripture to the body alone, since in death the body takes on the *appearance* of one who is asleep.[8]

First Thessalonians 4:13-17 is telling us that when Jesus comes again, He will bring *with* (Greek: *sun*) Him those whose bodies are "sleeping." To be more explicit, the souls and spirits of those who are now with Christ in glory will be reunited with their resurrection bodies (see 2 Corinthians 5:8; Philippians 1:22,23; 1 Corinthians 15). The Greek word *sun* indicates intimacy. The souls and spirits of the redeemed will be in a "side by side" position with Christ, and their physical bodies that are "sleeping" in the grave will in that instant be raised to immortality and reunited with their spirits.[9]

 If Jesus is bringing some believers "with" Him (verse 14), but they do not have resurrection bodies yet (verse 16), doesn't this mean the immaterial souls of these believers are "with" Jesus and will be reunited with their bodies at the Resurrection? This is an important issue to raise with Jehovah's Witnesses.

Philippians 1:21-23

"For to me, to live is Christ and to die is gain. If I am to go on living in the body, this will mean fruitful labor for me. Yet what shall I choose? I do not know! I am torn between the two: I desire to depart and be with Christ, which is far better." The question that immediately comes to mind is: How could Paul in his right mind refer to death as "gain" if death meant nonexistence? What Paul meant by "gain" is clear from the context, for he defines that gain as departing the physical body *to be with Christ*. Being with Christ is "far better" than remaining in the physical body. (Being in a state of nonexistence cannot be said to be "far better" by any stretch of the imagination.)

2 Corinthians 5:6-8

"Therefore, being always of good courage, and knowing that *while we are at home in the body we are absent from the Lord*— for we walk by faith, not by sight—we are of good courage, I say, and prefer rather *to be absent from the body and to be at home with the Lord*" (NASB, emphasis added).

The Greek word *pros* is used for the English word "with" in the phrase "be at home *with* the Lord." This word suggests close, face-to-face fellowship and intimate relationships. Paul thus indicates that the fellowship he expects to have with Christ immediately following his physical death will be one of great intimacy. Moreover, the Greek tenses in this passage indicate that the moment one is absent from the body, one is at home with the Lord. There is no lag period; it is an instant transition.

In view of such passages, Scripture is clear that man has an immaterial nature that consciously survives death.

Beware of how Jehovah's Witnesses interpret Luke 23:43. The New World Translation renders this verse, "And he said to him: 'Truly I tell you today, you will be with me in Paradise.'" This is in contrast to, for example, the New American Standard Bible which renders this verse, "Truly I say to you, today you shall be with Me in Paradise." I bring this to your attention because Luke 23:43 is a verse that supports conscious existence in the afterlife.

In the New World Translation, the comma is placed *after* the word "today," not after "you" as in the New American Standard Bible (and most other translations). The Watchtower Society does this to avoid the thief being with Jesus in paradise "today" (which implies conscious existence after death). Instead, they make it appear that Jesus' *statement* to the thief about paradise took place "today."

The phrase "truly, I say to you" occurs 74 times in the Gospels and is *always* used as an introductory expression by Jesus. It is similar to the Old Testament phrase "thus says the Lord."[10] Jesus used the "truly" phrase as a way of introducing an important truth. In 73 out of the 74 times the phrase occurs in the Gospels, the New World Translation (NWT) places a "break"—such as a comma—immediately after the phrase "truly, I tell you."[11] Luke 23:43 is the *only* occurrence of this phrase in which the NWT does not place a break after it. Why? Because if a break were placed after "truly, I say to you," the word "today" would then belong to the second half of the sentence, indicating that "today" the thief would be with Jesus in paradise.

 The verses Jehovah's Witnesses cite to prove that consciousness vanishes at death are taken out of context.

Psalm 146:3,4

As noted earlier, the New World Translation renders this passage, "Do not put your trust in nobles, nor in the son of earthling man, to whom no salvation belongs. His spirit goes out, he goes back to his ground; in that day *his thoughts do perish*" (emphasis added). This passage *does not* mean people will think no thoughts at all following the moment of death (see Revelation 6:9,10). In context and faithful to the original Hebrew,[12] it means that peoples' *plans, ambitions,* and *ideas for the future* will cease and come to naught at the moment of death. This is what the Hebrew word for "thoughts" communicates in Psalm 146:3,4. A person's plans and ideas for the future die with him or her. When John F. Kennedy died, for example, his plans and programs vanished with him.

Ecclesiastes 9:5

The New World Translation renders Ecclesiastes 9:5, "For the living are conscious that they will die; but as for the dead, *they are conscious of nothing at all*" (emphasis added). While the Watchtower Society interprets this as indicating a lack of consciousness following death,[13] the Bible teaches that the soul survives death in a state of conscious awareness (2 Corinthians 5:8). Contextually, Ecclesiastes 9:5 simply indicates that the dead know nothing so far as their bodily senses and worldly affairs are concerned (see also Ecclesiastes 9:6,10). But while the dead do not know what is happening *on earth*, they certainly do know what is going on *in heaven* (see Revelation 6:9,10) or in hell (see Luke 16:19-31).

In view of this, the Watchtower Society's use of Psalm 146:3,4 and Ecclesiastes 9:5 to "prove" there is no conscious existence in the afterlife is invalid.

Hell is a place of eternal conscious suffering for the wicked. The Scriptures use a variety of words to describe the horrors of hell, including fire, fiery furnace, unquenchable fire, the lake of burning sulfur, the Lake of Fire, everlasting contempt, perdition, the place of weeping and gnashing of teeth, eternal punishment, darkness, the wrath to come, torments, damnation, exclusion, condemnation, retribution, woe, and the second death (see, for example, Mark 9:43 and Revelation 14:11). *Hell is a horrible and real destiny.*

As awful as it is, there are many lines of biblical evidence that support the everlasting *consciousness* of the lost in hell:

- The rich man who died and went to hell was in conscious torment (Luke 16:22-28), and there is absolutely no indication in the text that it would ever cease.

- Jesus spoke repeatedly of the people in hell as "weeping and gnashing their teeth" (Matthew 8:12; 22:13; 24:51; 25:30), which necessitates awareness.

- Hell and heaven are "everlasting" (Matthew 25:46). [The same Greek word for "everlasting" *(aionion)* is used of both heaven and hell.]

- The fact that punishment is everlasting indicates that those being punished must be everlasting too. A person cannot suffer punishment unless he exists to be punished (2 Thessalonians 1:9). Annihilation, in the Jehovah's Witness view, must by definition take place *instantly*—in a mere moment. In view of this, it makes no sense to say the wicked will suffer "endless annihilation." Scripturally, the wicked will suffer a punishment that is everlasting—and this is a conscious punishment that will never end.

Hell

Hell was not part of God's original creation, which He called "very good" (Genesis 1:31). Hell was created later to confine Satan and the angels who rebelled against God (Matthew 25:41). Human beings who reject Christ will join Satan and his minions in this infernal place of suffering.

- Jesus repeatedly called hell a place of "unquenchable flames" (Mark 9:43-48) where the very bodies of the wicked will never die (see Luke 12:4,5). But it would make no sense to have everlasting flames torment bodies without souls.[14] Punishment cannot exist without consciousness.

- It cannot be denied that for someone who is suffering excruciating pain, the extinction of his or her consciousness would be a *blessing*—not a punishment (see Luke 23:30,31; Revelation 9:6).[15] Any honest seeker after truth must admit that "eternal punishment" cannot be defined as an extinction of consciousness.

- There are no degrees of annihilation, but Scripture reveals there will be degrees of suffering among the lost in hell (see Matthew 10:15; 11:21-24; 16:27; Luke 12:47,48; John 15:22; Hebrews 10:29; Revelation 20:11-15; 22:12). The fact that people will suffer varying degrees of punishment shows that annihilation or the extinction of consciousness is unbiblical.

- The beast and the false prophet are said to be thrown "alive" into the lake of fire at the beginning of Christ's thousand-year reign (Revelation 19:20), and they are still there, conscious and alive, *after* the 1,000 years has passed (20:10 NASB). This is the same as it will be for lost human beings.

How can the clear scriptural teaching that the wicked will suffer varying degrees of punishment in hell be reconciled with the Watchtower teaching of the annihilation of the wicked? And since the same Greek word for "eternal" in the phrase "eternal punishment" (Matthew 25:46) is used in the phrase "eternal life" (same verse), doesn't this indicate that the punishment of the wicked is just as eternal as the everlasting life of the righteous?

Man Is Conscious in the Afterlife; Hell Is a Place of Suffering

✓ The word "soul" has several important meanings, one of the most important being an immaterial nature that consciously survives death.

✓ Hell is not the grave but a place of *eternal conscious suffering* for the wicked.

For further information on refuting the Watchtower view of the afterlife, consult *Reasoning from the Scriptures with the Jehovah's Witnesses*, pp. 305-38.

Jesus Changed My Life
Forever

Giving your personal testimony of what the Lord Jesus has done in your life is a very important component of any witnessing encounter.

In my own case, throughout my childhood and teenage years I thought I was a Christian because I regularly attended church. For years I participated in various church activities, sang in the church choir, and went through all the motions. I even went through a "confirmation" ceremony at my church—an event that was supposed to confirm that I was a Christian. I had no idea at that time that I really wasn't a Christian according to the biblical definition.

Like so many others today, I was under the illusion that a Christian was a church-attender or someone who basically subscribed to a Christian code of ethics. I believed that as long as I was fairly consistent in living my life in accordance with this code of ethics, I was surely a Christian. I believed that as long as my good deeds outweighed my bad deeds by the time I died, I could look forward to a destiny in heaven.

It was years later when I came to understand that just going to church and living a "good" life didn't mean I was a Christian. As the great evangelist Billy Sunday (1862–1935) put it, "Going to church doesn't make you a Christian any more than going to a garage makes you an automobile."[1]

Fundamentally, a Christian is one who has a personal, ongoing relationship with Jesus. Christianity is not so much a *religion* as it is a *relationship*. It is a relationship that begins the moment someone places faith in Christ for salvation.

It is fascinating to me that the word "Christian" is used only three times in the New Testament—the most important of which is Acts 11:26 (see also Acts 26:28; 1 Peter 4:16). By observing what this word meant among those to whom the term was originally applied, we can see whether we are Christians according to biblical standards.

In Acts 11:26, we are told simply and straightforwardly, "The disciples were called Christians first at Antioch." This would have been around A.D. 42, about a decade after Christ died on the cross and resurrected from the dead. Up until this time the followers of Jesus had been known among themselves as "brothers" (Acts 15:1,23), "disciples" (Acts 9:26), "believers" (Acts 5:14 NASB), and "saints" (Romans 8:27).

What does "Christian" mean? The answer is found in the "ian" ending. Among the ancients, this ending meant "belonging to the party of." "Herodians" belonged to the party of Herod. "Caesarians" belonged to the party of Caesar. "Christians" belonged to Christ. And Christians were loyal to Christ just as the Herodians were loyal to Herod and Caesarians were loyal to Caesar (see Matthew 22:16; Mark 3:6; 12:13).

The significance of the name "Christian" was that these followers of Jesus were recognized as a distinct group. They were separate from Judaism and all other religions of the ancient world. We might loosely translate "Christians" as "those who belong to Christ," "Christ-ones," or perhaps "Christ-people." *They are ones who follow Christ.*

Imagine what it may have been like in Antioch as one local resident said something to another regarding these followers of Jesus.

"Who are these people?" one Antiochan might ask another. "Oh, they are the people who are always talking about Christ—the Christ-people, the Christians."

Those who have studied the culture of Antioch have noted that the Antiochans were well known for making fun of people. It may be that the early followers of Jesus were called "Christians" by local residents as a term of derision, an appellation of ridicule. Be that as it may, history reveals that by the second century Christians adopted the title as a badge of honor. They took pride (in a healthy kind of way) in following Jesus. They had a genuine relationship with the living, resurrected Christ, and they were utterly faithful to Him—even in the face of death.

In your personal testimony to a Jehovah's Witness, a pivotal part needs to include the fact that you are sure of going to heaven because you have a *personal relationship with Christ*. You have meaning in your present life not because you obey rules but because you have a *personal relationship with Christ*.

Great Christians throughout church history have long emphasized that Christianity involves a personal relationship.

- Josiah Strong (1847–1916) said, "Christianity is neither a creed nor a ceremonial, but life vitally connected with a loving Christ."[2]

- Stephen Neill (1900–1984) said, "Christianity is not the acceptance of certain ideas. It is a personal attitude of trust and devotion to a person."[3]

- John R.W. Stott (1921–) said, "A Christian is, in essence, somebody personally related to Jesus Christ."[4] He also said, "Christianity without Christ is a chest without a treasure, a frame without a portrait, a corpse without breath."[5]

- Oswald Chambers (1874–1917) said, "Christianity is not devotion to work, or to a cause, or a doctrine, but devotion to a person, the Lord Jesus Christ."[6]

- Billy Graham (born 1918) said, "Christianity isn't only going to church on Sunday. It is living twenty-four hours of every day with Jesus Christ."[7]

As you give your personal testimony, a key emphasis to continually bring up is that you are a Christian not because you do good works, not because you follow rules, not because you attend a particular church, not because you read a Bible. You are a Christian because you have a personal relationship with Jesus, the living Lord of the universe.

Having laid this basic foundation, here are a few pointers to keep in mind in regard to testimonies.

 There is a strong biblical precedent for God's people telling others about what God has done in their lives. Consider:

- "Give thanks to the LORD, call on his name; make known among the nations what he has done" (1 Chronicles 16:8).

- "Tell of all [God's] wonderful acts" (1 Chronicles 16:9).

- "Proclaim among the nations what [God] has done" (Psalm 9:11).

- "Let us tell in Zion what the LORD our God has done" (Jeremiah 51:10).

- "Whoever acknowledges me before men, I will also acknowledge him before my Father in heaven" (Matthew 10:32).

- Jesus said, "Go home to your family and tell them how much the Lord has done for you, and how he has had mercy on you. So the man went away and began to tell in the Decapolis how much Jesus had

done for him. And all the people were amazed"
(Mark 5:19,20).

- "You are witnesses of these things" (Luke 24:48).

- "Then, leaving her water jar, the woman went back
  to the town and said to the people, 'Come, see a
  man who told me everything I ever did. Could this
  be the Christ?' They came out of the town and
  made their way toward him....Many of the Samar-
  itans from that town believed in him because of the
  woman's testimony, 'He told me everything I ever
  did'" (John 4:28-30,39).

- "Do not be ashamed to testify about our Lord, or
  ashamed of me his prisoner. But join with me in
  suffering for the gospel, by the power of God"
  (2 Timothy 1:8).

- "Always be prepared to give an answer to everyone
  who asks you to give the reason for the hope that
  you have. But do this with gentleness and respect"
  (1 Peter 3:15).

***Christ has called us to be a "light" in the world around
us.*** Jesus said, "You are the light of the world. A city on
a hill cannot be hidden" (Matthew 5:14). He did not
call us to be "secret agent" Christians. We are not to cloak our
lights. Someone once said, "No one is a light unto himself, not
even the sun."[8] Because the darkness of the cults is hovering
over Western culture as never before, there has never been a
time when the light of each individual Christian has been more
needed. As evangelist Billy Graham put it, "The Christian
should stand out like a sparkling diamond."[9]

We are called to be personal witnesses of Jesus Christ. Just before ascending into heaven, Jesus instructed His disciples: "You will receive power when the Holy Spirit has come upon you; and you shall be My witnesses both in Jerusalem, and in all Judea and Samaria, and even to the remotest part of the earth" (Acts 1:8 NASB). A witness is a person who gives a testimony. Christians *testify about Jesus*—who He is and what He has done. They share about their personal relationship with Him.

A Christian leader once said, "Every heart with Christ is a missionary; every heart without Christ is a mission field." Christians can be witnessing missionaries wherever they are! And when the opportunity arises, we must be ready to share the good news.

 How You Live Is Important

It is not just our words that communicate our love for Jesus. Our actions, too, serve as a witness. What we believe as Christians affects the way we live. And when people around us notice this difference, it serves as a beacon to the fact that we are followers of Jesus. Don't just share the *facts* of your relationship with Jesus with a Jehovah's Witness; let him see the *effects* of that relationship in your life.

 When you tell others what the Lord has done in your life, speak with conviction. You may not be an authority about what every single verse in the Bible says, but *you are an authority* on what Jesus has personally done in your life. In our day of relativism—when there is so much confusion about so many things—a testimony delivered with conviction will be noticed. Just as the first-century Christians were bold in their witness for Christ, so must we be bold (see Acts 2:32; 3:15; 4:33; 13:30,31).

Don't have a spiritual chip on your shoulder. Being sensitive in how you share your testimony is crucial. If the Jehovah's Witness feels you are looking down on him or her because you have something he or she does not have, his or her attitude will turn off as fast as anything you can imagine.[10] It's easy to be overzealous when you have thoroughly prepared yourself by learning hard-hitting scriptural answers to Watchtower Society errors. Be careful to *converse with* the Jehovah's Witness. Make every effort, with God's help, to remain humble during your witnessing encounter. Watch out for spiritual pride; it is deadly!

 Share what your life was like before you were a Christian, how you became a Christian, and what your life has been like since becoming a Christian.

- Describe what your life was like before you were a Christian. What were your feelings, attitudes, actions, and relationships like during this time? (The apostle Paul clearly spoke of what his life was like before he was a Christian— Acts 26:4-11.)

- What events transpired in your life that led to your decision to trust in Christ? What caused you to begin considering Him as a solution to your needs? Was there a crisis? A lack of meaning in life? Be specific.

- Describe your conversion experience. Was it a book you read? Were you in a church? Were other Christians with you at the time? (The apostle Paul clearly spoke of how he became a Christian—Acts 26:12-18.)

- What kind of change took place in your life following your conversion? What effect did trusting in Christ have on your feelings, attitudes, actions, and relationships? (Paul spoke of how his life changed after he became a Christian—Acts 26:19-23.)

There are certain things to avoid when sharing your personal testimony.

- *Don't be long-winded.* People have short attention spans. Unless they indicate they want every detail, cover the essential points in a brief fashion.

- *Stay away from "Christianese" language.* Do not use theological language your listener may be unfamiliar with, such as justification, reconciliation, and sanctification. If you do use these words, be sure to clearly define what you mean by them.

- *Do not communicate that Christianity yields a bed of roses for believers.* Such a claim is simply not true. You might even share some of the struggles you have gone through since becoming a Christian. Your listener may identify with what you have experienced.

- *Do not be insensitive to the Jehovah's Witness' "works" background.* The apostle Paul stated: "A natural man does not accept the things of the Spirit of God, for they are foolishness to him; and he cannot understand them, because they are spiritually appraised" (1 Corinthians 2:14 NASB). The gospel of God's grace may not make much sense to someone who has been thoroughly schooled in a "gospel" that involves works. For this reason, devote a good part of your testimony to how the gospel of God's grace has set you free.

As you close your testimony, leave the Jehovah's Witness with a clear picture of how to become a Christian. The following are the most important points to make.

God Desires a Personal Relationship with Human Beings

God created human beings (Genesis 1:27). And He did not create them to exist apart from Him. He created people with a view to coming into a personal relationship with Him.

God had face-to-face encounters and fellowship with Adam and Eve, the first couple (Genesis 3:8-19). Just as God fellowshiped with them, so He desires to fellowship with us. God *loves* us (John 3:16; 1 John 1:5-9).

The problem is...

Humanity Has a Sin Problem that Blocks a Relationship with God

When Adam and Eve chose to sin against God in the Garden of Eden, they catapulted the entire human race—to which they gave birth—into sin. Since the time of Adam and Eve, *every* human being has been born into the world with a propensity to sin. The apostle Paul affirmed that "sin entered the world through one man, and death through sin" (Romans 5:12). Indeed, we are told that "through the disobedience of the one man the many were made sinners" (Romans 5:19). This means that "death came through a man...in Adam all die" (1 Corinthians 15:21,22).

Jesus often spoke of sin in metaphors that illustrate the havoc sin wreaks in life. He described sin as blindness (Matthew 23:16-26), sickness (Matthew 9:12), being enslaved in bondage (John 8:34), and living in darkness (John 8:12; 12:35-46). Moreover, Jesus taught that this is a *universal* condition, and all people are guilty before God (Luke 7:37-48).

Our Lord also taught that both inner thoughts and external acts render a person guilty (Matthew 5:28). He taught that from within the human heart come "evil thoughts, sexual immorality, theft, murder, adultery, greed, malice, deceit, lewdness, envy, slander, arrogance, and folly" (Mark 7:21,22). He also affirmed that God is fully aware of *every* person's sins, both external acts and inner thoughts; nothing escapes His notice (Matthew 22:18; Luke 6:8; John 4:17-19).

Many people, including some Jehovah's Witnesses, believe that "clean" living is the way to heaven. It's important to discuss that even if we try to live a life of consistent good works, *we all fall short of God's infinite standards* (Romans 3:23). Here's a good illustration: In a contest to see who can throw a rock to the moon, I am sure a muscular athlete would be able to throw a rock much farther than I could. But all human beings ultimately fall short of the task. Similarly, all of us fall short of measuring up to God's perfect holy standards.

Though the sin problem is a serious one, God has graciously provided a solution...

Jesus Died for Our Sins and Made Salvation Possible

God's absolute holiness demands that sin be punished. The good news of the gospel, however, is that Jesus has taken this entire punishment on Himself. God loves us so much that He sent Jesus to bear the full weight of the penalty for our sins!

It is critical that you help the Jehovah's Witness understand what Scripture says about this. Jesus affirmed that it was for the very purpose of dying that He came into the world (John 12:27). He perceived His death as being a sacrificial offering *for the sins of humanity* (Matthew 26:26-28). Jesus took His sacrificial mission with utmost seriousness, for He knew that without Him humanity would certainly perish (Matthew 16:25; John 3:16) and spend eternity apart from God in a place of great suffering (Matthew 10:28; 11:23; Luke 16:22-28).

Jesus described His mission this way: "The Son of Man did not come to be served, but to serve, and to give his life as a ransom for many" (Matthew 20:28); "the Son of Man came to seek and to save what was lost" (Luke 19:10). "God did not send his Son into the world to condemn the world, but to save the world through him" (John 3:17). (To understand the truth of Jesus as a "ransom," review chapter 7—"Salvation Is by Grace Through Faith, Not by Works.")

Believe in Jesus Christ

It is critical to understand that the benefits of Christ's death on the cross are not automatically applied to our lives. By His sacrificial death on the cross, Jesus took the sins of the entire world on Himself and made salvation available for everyone (1 John 2:2). But this salvation is not automatic. *Only those who choose to believe in Christ are saved.* This is the consistent testimony of the biblical Jesus. "For God so loved the world that he gave his one and only Son, that whoever *believes* in him shall not perish but have eternal life" (John 3:16, emphasis added). "I am the resurrection and the life. He who *believes* in me will live, even though he dies" (John 11:25, emphasis added). *Faith in Christ brings salvation,* not obedience to Watchtower Society rules.

Choosing not to believe in Jesus, by contrast, leads to eternal condemnation: "Whoever *believes* in him is not condemned, but whoever *does not believe* stands condemned already because he has not believed in the name of God's one and only Son" (John 3:18, emphasis added).

Free at Last: Forgiven of All Sins

When a person believes in Christ the Savior, a wonderful thing happens. God forgives him or her of all sin. *Every one of them!* He puts them completely out of His sight. Be sure to share the following verses, which speak of the forgiveness of those who have believed in Christ:

- "In him we have redemption through his blood, the forgiveness of sins, in accordance with the riches of God's grace" (Ephesians 1:7).

- God said, "Their sins and lawless acts I will remember no more" (Hebrews 10:17).

- "Blessed is he whose transgressions are forgiven, whose sins are covered. Blessed is the man whose sin the LORD does not count against him and in whose spirit is no deceit" (Psalm 32:1,2).

- "For as high as the heavens are above the earth, so great is his love for those who fear him; as far as the east is from the west, so far has he removed our transgressions from us" (Psalm 103:11,12).

Such forgiveness is wonderful indeed because *none of us* can work our way into salvation or be good enough to warrant God's favor. Because of what Jesus has done for us, we freely receive the gift of salvation through Him. It is a gift provided solely through the grace of God (Ephesians 2:8,9). And all of this is ours by simply believing in Jesus.

Don't Put It Off!

Help your Jehovah's Witness acquaintance see that it is dangerous to put off turning to Christ for salvation, for no one knows the day of his or her death. "Death is the destiny of every man; the living should take this to heart" (Ecclesiastes 7:2). "Seek the LORD while he may be found; call on him while he is near" (Isaiah 55:6).

A Simple Prayer of Faith

If the Jehovah's Witness to whom you are speaking expresses interest in trusting in *Jesus alone* for salvation (having understood the *true* scriptural teaching on Jesus and the gospel), you might lead him or her in a simple prayer like the following. Be sure to emphasize that it is not the prayer that saves anyone; it is *faith in Jesus* that brings salvation.

> *Dear Jesus,*
> *I want to have a relationship with You.*
> *I know I can't save myself because I'm a sinner.*
> *I believe You died on the cross for me. Thank You.*
> *I accept Your free gift of salvation.*
> *Thank You, Jesus.*
> *Amen.*

Welcome the Jehovah's Witness into God's Forever Family!

On the authority of the Word of God, you can now assure the Jehovah's Witness that he or she is part of God's forever family. Encourage him or her with the prospect of spending eternity by the side of Jesus in heaven!

 For further information on witnessing to Jehovah's Witnesses, consult *Reasoning from the Scriptures with the Jehovah's Witnesses*, pp. 9-21, 403-08.

 An Exhortation. The Jehovah's Witness you've led to Christ *still needs your assistance!* Help him get grounded in a good, Bible-believing church. Introduce him to some of your Christian friends, and have your friends pray for him regularly. Realize that he may be carrying some psychological and spiritual "baggage" from his past association with the Watchtower Society. Help him work through this. If there is a Christian support group for former Jehovah's Witnesses in your area, check it out as a possible support for this new Christian.

Bibliography

1980 Yearbook of Jehovah's Witnesses. Brooklyn: Watchtower Bible and Tract Society, 1980.

Abanes, Richard. *Cults, New Religious Movements, and Your Family*. Wheaton, IL: Crossway, 1998.

Aid to Bible Understanding. Brooklyn: Watchtower Bible and Tract Society, 1971.

Ankerberg, John and John Weldon. *Cult Watch: What You Need to Know About Spiritual Deception*. Eugene, OR: Harvest House Publishers, 1991.

_____. *Encyclopedia of Cults and New Religions*. Eugene, OR: Harvest House Publishers, 1999.

Beliefs of Other Kinds: A Guide to Interfaith Witness in the United States. Atlanta: Baptist Home Mission Board, 1984.

Blood, Medicine, and the Law of God. Brooklyn: Watchtower Bible and Tract Society, 1961.

Boa, Kenneth. *Cults, World Religions, and You*. Wheaton, IL: Victor Books, 1979.

Bowman, Robert M. *Jehovah's Witnesses*. Grand Rapids: Zondervan Publishing House, 1995.

_____. *Why You Should Believe in the Trinity*. Grand Rapids: Baker Book House, 1989.

Chretien, Leonard and Marjorie. *Witnesses of Jehovah*. Eugene, OR: Harvest House Publishers, 1988.

Enroth, Ronald. *A Guide to Cults and New Religions*. Downers Grove, IL: InterVarsity Press, 1983.

_____. *The Lure of the Cults*. Downers Grove, IL: InterVarsity Press, 1987.

The Finished Mystery. Brooklyn: Watchtower Bible and Tract Society, 1917.

Gerstner, John H. *The Theology of the Major Sects*. Grand Rapids: Baker Book House, 1980.

Gomes, Alan. *Unmasking the Cults*. Grand Rapids: Zondervan Publishing House, 1995.

Halverson, Dean C., ed. *The Compact Guide to World Religions*. Minneapolis: Bethany House Publishers, 1996.

The Harp of God. Brooklyn: Watchtower Bible and Tract Society, 1921.

Hoekema, Anthony A. *The Four Major Cults*. Grand Rapids: Eerdmans, 1978.

Jehovah's Witnesses and the Question of Blood. Brooklyn: Watchtower Bible and Tract Society, 1977.

Jehovah's Witnesses: Proclaimers of God's Kingdom. Brooklyn: Watchtower Bible and Tract Society, 1993.

Jehovah's Witnesses: The Organization Behind the Name. Brooklyn: Watchtower Bible and Tract Society, 1990.

"The Kingdom Is at Hand." Brooklyn: Watchtower Bible and Tract Society, 1944.

"Let God Be True." Brooklyn: Watchtower Bible and Tract Society, 1946.

"Let Your Name Be Sanctified." Brooklyn: Watchtower Bible and Tract Society, 1961.

Life Everlasting—In Freedom of the Sons of God. Brooklyn: Watchtower Bible and Tract Society, 1966.

Life—How Did It Get Here? Brooklyn: Watchtower Bible and Tract Society, 1985.

Magnani, Duane. *The Watchtower Files*. Minneapolis: Bethany House Publishers, 1985.

Making Your Family Life Happy. Brooklyn: Watchtower Bible and Tract Society, 1978.

Mankind's Search for God. Brooklyn: Watchtower Bible and Tract Society, 1990.

Man's Salvation Out of World Distress at Hand! Brooklyn: Watchtower Bible and Tract Society, 1975.

Martin, Paul. *Cult-Proofing Your Kids*. Grand Rapids: Zondervan Publishing House, 1993.

Martin, Walter. *The Kingdom of the Cults*. Minneapolis: Bethany House Publishers, 1999.

_____. *Martin Speaks Out on the Cults*. Ventura, CA: Regal Books, 1983.

_____. *The New Cults*. Ventura, CA: Regal Books, 1980.

_____. *The Rise of the Cults*. Ventura, CA: Regal Books, 1983.

Martin, Walter and Norman Klann. *Jehovah of the Watchtower*. Minneapolis: Bethany House Publishers, 1974.

Mather, George A. and Larry A. Nichols. *Dictionary of Cults, Sects, Religions and the Occult*. Grand Rapids: Zondervan Publishing House, 1993.

McDowell, Josh, and Don Stewart. *Handbook of Today's Religions*. San Bernardino: Here's Life Publishers, 1989.

_____. *Understanding the Cults*. San Bernardino, CA: Here's Life Publishers, 1983.

The New World. Brooklyn: Watchtower Bible and Tract Society, 1942.

Paradise Restored to Mankind—By Theocracy. Brooklyn: Watchtower Bible and Tract Society, 1972.

Pement, Eric, ed. *Contend for the Faith*. Chicago: EMNR, 1992.

Qualified to be Ministers. Brooklyn: Watchtower Bible and Tract Society, 1955.

Reasoning from the Scriptures. Brooklyn: Watchtower Bible and Tract Society, 1989.

Reconciliation. Brooklyn: Watchtower Bible and Tract Society, 1928.

Reed, David. *Blood on the Altar.* Amherst, NY: Prometheus Books, 1996.

_____. *How to Rescue Your Loved One from the Watchtower.* Grand Rapids: Baker Book House, 1989.

_____. *Jehovah's Witnesses Answered Verse by Verse.* Grand Rapids: Baker Book House, 1992.

_____. *Jehovah's Witness Literature.* Grand Rapids: Baker Book House, 1993.

Rhodes, Ron. *The Complete Book of Bible Answers.* Eugene, OR: Harvest House Publishers, 1999.

_____. *Jehovah's Witnesses: What You Need to Know.* Eugene, OR: Harvest House Publishers, 1999.

_____. *Reasoning from the Scriptures with the Jehovah's Witnesses.* Eugene, OR: Harvest House Publishers, 1993.

Riches. Brooklyn: Watchtower Bible and Tract Society, 1936.

Robertson, Irvine. *What the Cults Believe.* Chicago: Moody Press, 1983.

Saliba, John A. *Understanding New Religious Movements.* Grand Rapids: Eerdmans, 1995.

Should You Believe in the Trinity? Brooklyn: Watchtower Bible and Tract Society, 1989.

Sire, James. *Scripture Twisting.* Downers Grove, IL: InterVarsity Press, 1980.

Studies in the Scriptures. Brooklyn: Watchtower Bible and Tract Society, 1897.

Swenson, Orville. *The Perilous Path of Cultism.* Saskatchewan, CN: Briercrest Books, 1987.

"Things in Which It Is Impossible for God to Lie." Brooklyn: Watchtower Bible and Tract Society, 1965.

Tucker, Ruth. *Another Gospel: Alternative Religions and the New Age Movement.* Grand Rapids: Zondervan Publishing House, 1989.

You Can Live Forever in Paradise on Earth. Brooklyn: Watchtower Bible and Tract Society, 1982.

"Your Will Be Done on Earth." Brooklyn: Watchtower Bible and Tract Society, 1958.

Notes

Chapter 1

1. *The Watchtower,* 1 December 1981, p. 27.
2. *The Watchtower,* 15 June 1957, p. 370.
3. *The Watchtower,* 15 January 1983, p. 22.
4. David Reed, *Jehovah's Witnesses Answered Verse by Verse* (Grand Rapids: Baker, 1992), p. 121.
5. *Reasoning from the Scriptures* (Brooklyn: Watchtower Bible and Tract Society, 1989), p. 205.
6. Robert M. Bowman, *Understanding Jehovah's Witnesses* (Grand Rapids: Baker, 1991), p. 62.
7. *Your Will Be Done on Earth* (Brooklyn: Watchtower Bible and Tract Society, 1958), p. 362.
8. *Vine's Expository Dictionary of Biblical Words* (Nashville: Thomas Nelson, 1985), p. 330.
9. Michael Green, *The Second Epistle of Peter and the Epistle of Jude* (Grand Rapids: Eerdmans, 1979), p. 91.
10. *Studies in the Scriptures,* vol. 2 (Brooklyn: Watchtower Bible and Tract Society, 1888), pp. 98-99.
11. *Millions Now Living Will Never Die* (Brooklyn: Watchtower Bible and Tract Society, 1920), pp. 88-90.
12. *Awake!* magazine, 8 October 1966, p. 19.
13. *Golden Age,* 4 February 1931, p. 293.
14. *Awake!* 22 August 1965, p. 20.
15. David Reed, *How to Rescue Your Loved One from the Watch Tower* (Grand Rapids: Baker Book House, 1989), pp. 104-06.
16. *The Watchtower,* 15 November 1967, pp. 702-04.
17. *Awake!* 8 June 1968, p. 21.
18. *The Watchtower,* 15 March 1980, p. 31.
19. John Ankerberg and John Weldon, *The Facts on Jehovah's Witnesses* (Eugene, OR: Harvest House Publishers, 1988), p. 7.
20. See David Reed, *Blood on the Altar* (New York: Prometheus, 1996), p. 137.
21. Ankerberg and Weldon, *Facts,* p. 7.

Chapter 2

1. Julius R. Mantey, cited in Erich and Jean Grieshaber, *Exposé of Jehovah's Witnesses* (Tyler: Jean Books, 1982), p. 30.
2. Bruce Metzger, *Theology Today,* April 1953.
3. William Barclay, *The Expository Times,* November 1953.
4. Robert H. Countess, *The Jehovah's Witnesses New Testament* (Phillipsburg, NJ: Presbyterian and Reformed, 1982), p. 91.
5. Ibid.
6. Ibid.
7. Raymond Franz, *Crisis of Conscience* (Atlanta: Commentary Press, 1983), p. 50, note 15.
8. Walter Martin, *The Kingdom of the Cults* (Minneapolis: Bethany, 1974), p. 124.
9. *The Watchtower,* March 1880, p. 83.
10. Ibid., 15 May 1892, p. 1410.
11. Ibid., 15 July 1959, p. 421.
12. Ibid., November 1964, p. 671.
13. *Reasoning from the Scriptures* (Brooklyn: Watchtower Bible and Tract Society, 1989), p. 409.
14. Robert Bowman, *Understanding Jehovah's Witnesses* (Grand Rapids: Baker, 1991), p. 66.
15. Jerry and Marian Bodine, *Witnessing to the Witnesses* (Irvine, CA: n.p., n.d.), pp. 39-40.
16. Ibid., p. 40.
17. *The Watchtower,* 7 December 1995, p. 4.
18. *Reasoning from the Scriptures,* p. 212.
19. Julius Mantey, *Christian Research Newsletter,* 3:3, p. 5.
20. *Reasoning from the Scriptures,* p. 421.

Chapter 3

1. Marian Bodine, *Christian Research Newsletter,* May/June 1992, p. 3.
2. Ibid.
3. This is not to deny that the Jehovah's Witnesses can point to some manuscripts that contain the name "Jehovah." A few copies of the Septuagint, the Greek translation of the Hebrew Old Testament, use Jehovah. But such manuscripts are not held to be reliable. The majority of the manuscripts know nothing of this name.
4. Robert Bowman, *Why You Should Believe in the Trinity* (Grand Rapids: Baker, 1989), p. 110.

5. *Reasoning from the Scriptures* (Brooklyn: Watchtower Bible and Tract Society, 1989), p. 195.
6. David Reed, *Jehovah's Witnesses Answered Verse by Verse* (Grand Rapids: Baker, 1992), p. 34.
7. Bowman, *Why*, p. 110.
8. Ibid., p. 113.
9. Ibid., p. 117.
10. Reed, *Jehovah's Witnesses*, p. 29.
11. Ibid., p. 52.
12. Robert Bowman, *Understanding Jehovah's Witnesses* (Grand Rapids: Baker, 1991), pp. 120-21 and *Why You Should Believe in the Trinity*, p. 108.
13. Bodine, *Christian Research Newsletter*, p. 3.

Chapter 4

1. *The Watchtower*, 15 August 1987, p. 29.
2. *You Can Live Forever in Paradise on Earth* (Brooklyn: Watchtower, 1982), p. 143.
3. *Aid to Bible Understanding* (Brooklyn: Watchtower, 1971), p. 1395.
4. Robert Reymond, *Jesus, Divine Messiah* (Phillipsburg, NJ: Presbyterian and Reformed, 1990), p. 247.
5. Robert Bowman, *Why You Should Believe in the Trinity* (Grand Rapids: Baker, 1989), p. 77.
6. *Reasoning from the Scriptures* (Brooklyn: Watchtower, 1989), p. 342.

Chapter 5

1. *Should You Believe in the Trinity?* (Brooklyn: Watchtower Bible and Tract Society, 1989), p. 20.
2. *Reasoning from the Scriptures* (Brooklyn: Watchtower Bible and Tract Society, 1989), p. 380.
3. Ibid., p. 407.
4. William Arndt and Wilbur Gingrich, *A Greek-English Lexicon of the New Testament and Other Early Christian Literature* (Chicago: University of Chicago Press, 1957), p. 874.
5. Ibid., p. 146.
6. *Should You Believe in the Trinity?* p. 21.
7. Ibid.
8. Ibid., p. 22.
9. Robert Bowman, *Why You Should Believe in the Trinity* (Grand Rapids: Baker, 1989), p. 115.

Chapter 6

1. *Reconciliation* (Brooklyn: Watchtower Bible and Tract Society, 1928), p. 101.
2. Walter Martin, *Jehovah of the Watchtower* (Minneapolis: Bethany House, 1974), p. 43.
3. *Studies in the Scripture*, vol. 5 (Brooklyn: Watchtower Bible and Tract Society, 1899), pp. 60-61.
4. Ibid., p. 76.
5. "Let God Be True" (Brooklyn: Watchtower Bible and Tract Society, 1946), p. 102, emphasis added.
6. Benjamin B. Warfield, *The Person and Work of Christ* (Philadelphia: Presbyterian and Reformed Publishing Co., 1950), p. 66.
7. Cited in ibid.
8. Paul G. Weathers, "Answering the Arguments of Jehovah's Witnesses Against the Trinity," in *Contend for the Faith*, ed. Eric Pement (Chicago: EMNR, 1992), p. 136.

Chapter 7

1. *The Watchtower* magazine, 1 April 1947, p. 204.
2. Ibid., 15 August 1972, p. 491.
3. *Reasoning from the Scriptures* (Brooklyn: Watchtower Bible and Tract Society, 1989), p. 308.
4. Duane Magnani, *The Watchtower Files* (Minneapolis: Bethany, 1985), p. 232.
5. Ibid., p. 77.
6. J.H. Thayer, *A Greek-English Lexicon of the New Testament* (Grand Rapids, MI: Zondervan, 1963), p. 50
7. Spiros Zodhiates, *The Complete Word Study Dictionary* (Chattanooga, TN: AMG Pumblishers, 1992), p. 193.
8. *Should You Believe in the Trinity?* (Brooklyn: Watchtower Bible and Tract Society, 1989), p. 16.
9. Adapted from *The Ryrie Study Bible* (Chicago: Moody Press, 1986), p. 1622.
10. *The Wycliffe Bible Commentary* (Chicago: Moody Press, 1974), p. 1325.
11. The NIV Study Bible, ed. Kenneth Barker (Grand Rapids: Zondervan, 1985), p. 1806.
12. Ryrie Study Bible, p. 1614.

Chapter 8

1. *Reasoning from the Scriptures* (Brooklyn: Watchtower Bible and Tract Society, 1989), p. 76.
2. Ibid., p. 79.
3. Ibid., pp. 166-67.
4. *The New Treasury of Scripture Knowledge,* ed. Jerome Smith (Nashville: Thomas Nelson, 1992), p. 1516.
5. Ibid., p. 482.
6. Ibid., pp. 482-83.
7. Charles C. Ryrie, *Revelation* (Chicago: Moody Press, 1981), p. 51.
8. Norman Geisler and Thomas Howe, *When Critics Ask* (Wheaton, IL: Victor Books, 1992), p. 554.
9. David Reed, *Jehovah's Witnesses Answered Verse by Verse* (Grand Rapids: Baker, 1992), p. 79.
10. *The Wycliffe Bible Commentary,* eds. Charles F. Pfeiffer and Everett F. Harrison (Chicago: Moody Press, 1974), p. 1078.
11. William F. Arndt and F. Wilbur Gingrich, *A Greek-Lexicon of the New Testament and Other Early Christian Literature* (Chicago: University of Chicago Press, 1957) p. 270
12. Reed, *Jehovah's Witnesses Answered,* pp. 33-34.
13. *New Treasury,* p. 610.
14. NIV Study Bible, ed. Kenneth Barker (Grand Rapids: Zondervan, 1985), p. 822.
15. *Theological Wordbook of the Old Testament,* ed. R. Laird Harris, vol. 2 (Chicago: Moody Press, 1981), p. 645.

Chapter 9

1. *Reasoning from the Scriptures* (Brooklyn: Watchtower Bible and Tract Society, 1989), p. 384.
2. *You Can Live Forever in Paradise on Earth* (Brooklyn: Watchtower Bible and Tract Society, 1982), p. 88.
3. Ibid., p. 83.
4. Francis Brown, S. Driver, and Charles Briggs, *A Hebrew and English Lexicon of the Old Testament* (Oxford: Clarendon Press, 1980), p. 659.
5. H. Leupold, *Exposition of Genesis,* vol. 2 (Grand Rapids: Baker, 1968), p. 924.
6. Ibid.
7. William Arndt and Wilbur Gingrich, *A Greek-English Lexicon of the New Testament* (Chicago: University of Chicago Press, 1957), pp. 681-83.
8. Walter Martin, "Jehovah's Witnesses and the Doctrine of Death," *Christian Research Newsletter,* 5:3, p. 4.
9. Ibid.
10. Robert M. Bowman, *Understanding Jehovah's Witnesses* (Grand Rapids: Baker, 1991), pp. 99-100.
11. Ibid.
12. *Theological Wordbook of the Old Testament,* ed. Laird Harris (Chicago: Moody, 1980), 2:1056.
13. *Reasoning from the Scriptures,* p. 169.
14. Alan Gomes, "Evangelicals and the Annihilation of Hell," part 2, *Christian Research Journal,* Summer 1991, p. 11.
15. William G.T. Shedd, cited in ibid., p. 18.

Chapter 10

1. *Draper's Book of Quotations for the Christian World* (Grand Rapids: Baker, 1992), p. 73.
2. Ibid., p. 65.
3. *More Gathered Gold,* electronic media, HyperCard stack.
4. Ibid.
5. Ibid.
6. *Draper's,* p. 66.
7. Ibid.
8. *More Gathered Gold.*
9. Ibid.
10. Walter Martin, "The Do's and Don'ts of Witnessing to Cultists," *Christian Research Newsletter,* January–February 1992, p. 4.